LIVING A LIFE THAT MATTERS

LESSONS FROM SOLOMON
THE MAN WHO TRIED EVERYTHING

Mark Matlock with Christopher Lyon

ZONDERVAN®

Youth Specialties
www.youthspecialties.com

www.invertbooks.com

ZONDERVAN.com/
AUTHORTRACKER
follow your favorite authors

Living a Life that Matters: Lessons from Solomon - the man who tried everything
Copyright © 2005 by Youth Specialties

Youth Specialties products, 300 S. Pierce St., El Cajon, CA 92020 are published
by Zondervan, 5300 Patterson Ave. SE, Grand Rapids, MI 49530.

Library of Congress Cataloging-in-Publication Data

Matlock, Mark.
  Living a life that matters : lessons from Solomon- the man who tried
everything / by Mark Matlock.
      p. cm.
    ISBN-10: 0-310-25816-2 (pbk.)
    ISBN-13: 978-0-310-25816-2 (pbk.)
    1. Christian youth—Religious life. 2. Bible. O.T.
Ecclesiastes—Criticism, interpretation, etc. I. Title.
    BV4531.3.M39 2005
    248.8'3—dc22

                                                              2005015116

Web site addresses listed in this book were current at the time of publication.
Please contact Youth Specialties via e-mail (YS@YouthSpecialties.com) to report
URLs that are no longer operational and replacement URLs if available.

Editorial direction by Randy Southern
Edited by Sharon Odegaard
Proofread by Anna Hammond and Heather Haggerty
Cover design by Burnkit
Interior design by SharpSeven Design

Printed in the United States of America

06 07 08 09 10 11 12 • 19 18 17 16 15 14 13 12 11 10 9 8 7 6 5 4 3 2

THIS BOOK IS DEDICATED TO MY PARENTS, TOM AND JUDI MATLOCK WHO TAUGHT ME HOW TO LOOK AROUND AND SEE GOD'S TRUTH EVERYWHERE.

CONTENTS

HOW TO USE
HOW TO USE THIS BOOK
THIS BOOK

Have you ever been driving on the highway past some really beautiful scenery? Maybe it was the mountains or a gorgeous coastline? You can respond to that kind of drive in one of two ways. Either keep your foot on the gas and just try to catch glimpses while you speed past. Or stop once in a while to take it all in. Maybe snap a few pictures. Some people even like to get off the highway and explore the backroads to get a real flavor for the country.

You can read a book like this in one of two ways, also. Lots of people will pick it up and just plow through the pages from front to back. They might like some of the ideas that whiz by, but they don't have time to really stop and think about it.

We hope some of you take the other approach to these pages. Getting the most out of it probably means taking some time as you read for reflection about what you're reading and how it fits with what you're seeing in the world around you. It's tough to wrestle with deep truths about who you are and where your life is headed without slowing down a little.

OBSERVATION EXERCISES

To help, we've provided some "scenic overlooks" at the end of each chapter. They're called "Observation Exercises." The idea is to pull off for a few minutes, get out, stretch your mental legs, and really notice how the ideas in the book match up with what you're seeing in your own world. And then to think about what you should do about it.

HOW TO TALK TO UNBELIEVING FRIENDS

If you're a believer, take a minute while your stopped to look at our suggestions for talking to someone who isn't a Christian about what you've just read. Our hope is to give you enough juice to jumpstart a conversation about the most important things in life with your friends and family members.

TOO MUCH IS

TOO MUCH IS NEVER ENOUGH

NEVER ENOUGH

What if you could have it all?

Money. Power. Love. Sex. Respect. Popularity. Absolutely anything you want. Many of us spend our lives wishing for that very scenario—or at least imagining what it would be like. But not many of us get there.

Mel Gibson got there.

Once an unknown Australian actor, Gibson got his first big break starring in the cult classic *Mad Max* when he was twenty-three. More big roles followed in blockbusters such as the *Lethal Weapon* series, *Maverick, Ransom, Conspiracy Theory, Payback, What Women Want* and *Signs.* As his international stardom grew, so did his bank account. He is now one of the top-paid actors in the world. For every movie he stars in, he now gets $25 million.

But acting wasn't enough for him. In 1993 he stepped behind the camera to direct *The Man Without a Face.* Two years later he earned two Academy Awards for directing and producing *Braveheart.*

Gibson's success didn't stop with his career. He's been married to the same woman for 25 years, and they have seven kids together. *People* magazine named him the Sexiest Man Alive. *Premiere* magazine listed him as one of the most powerful people in Hollywood.

Worldwide fame. Unlimited riches. True love. Fatherhood. Widespread respect for his talent. International renown for his sexual appeal. Virtually limitless power in his career. Rarely does one man get so much in one lifetime.

Mel Gibson had it all. So he must have been the happiest man on the planet, right? He had the power to do almost anything he wanted. The money to buy almost anything he could imagine. Almost nothing was out of reach for him.

Yet Gibson felt something was missing. All that he had wasn't enough for him. So he added some new experiences to the mix. "I would get addicted to anything," he admits. "Anything at all, okay? Drugs, booze, anything. You name it. Coffee, cigarettes. Sometimes I used to drive inebriated. I mean, this is the height of careless stupidity. Done a lot of things I'm not proud of."

Eventually Gibson sought treatment for his addictions. But after getting clean and sober, he found himself right back where he had started: with an emptiness in his life.

"I just didn't want to go on."

That's what he told Diane Sawyer in an interview on ABC's *Primetime Live*. All of his personal success had brought him to a place where the most appealing option to him was to jump out a window and end it all.

"You know, I was looking down thinking, man, this is just easier this way," he said. "I don't know, you have to be mad, you have to be insane to despair in that way. But that is the height of spiritual bankruptcy. There's nothing left."

NOTHING WORKS

If Mel Gibson had made that jump—if he'd killed himself at the height of his success—he would have joined a list of well-known people who "got it all" and then decided it wasn't enough. One of the best known is Nirvana's Kurt Cobain. He and his band turned the music world upside down in the early 1990s with what became known as grunge music. They enjoyed enormous success with critics and music lovers alike. Despite that success, Cobain refused to become a corporate icon and stayed true to his "slacker" roots. And a generation of fans loved him for it.

Worldwide fame. Big money. Artistic respect. Influential power. Love (Courtney that is). Integrity. Fatherhood. Drugs. Alcohol. Sex. Kurt Cobain had it all. But all of it wasn't enough to help him overcome his lifelong battle with depression, addiction, and chronic pain. In fact, some people who knew him said having it all might have made things worse. Eventually, he just couldn't enjoy any of it.

A note he had written shortly before his apparent suicide offered some clues about the burden his success had become: "I've tried everything within my power to appreciate it (and I do, God, believe me I do, but it's not enough).... I need to be slightly numb in order to regain the enthusiasms I once had as a child." Later he wrote, "I don't have the passion anymore, and so remember, it's better to burn out than to fade away."

Trent Reznor knows what it's like to have it all, too. The world-famous front man for the band Nine Inch Nails is respected by fans of industrial metal music for honestly expressing his rage and despair at life's injustice and emptiness. Reznor's lyrics describe his sometimes shocking, usually depressing, views on everything from relationships to sex to religion to love.

Worldwide fame. Big money. Love from black-clad fans and music critics. Power. Drugs. Alcohol. Sex. Reznor has almost everything anyone could possibly want out of life. And here's what he said about it: "It didn't make sense...nothing brought me joy. After I got everything I ever wanted, I was ****ing worse off than I was before."

Something's not adding up here, is it?

If getting everything life has to offer doesn't bring happiness or peace or joy, what's the point of living? That's the question Mel Gibson, Kurt Cobain, and Trent Reznor—as well as countless other rich and successful people—came face to face with. Those guys got to a place most of us never will. They made their fantasies reality. They indulged in everything life has to offer—alcohol, drugs, sex, art. You name it, they tried it.

And what conclusion did they reach? Nothing satisfies. Not in the long run, at least. Not in a way that matters.

They weren't the first guys to reach that depressing conclusion. In fact the viewpoint is as ancient as the Old Testament. A poet-king named Solomon reached the same conclusion about life on earth 3,000 years ago. In a book called Ecclesiastes, he spells out everything he tried in his quest for meaning in this life—and how all of it left him feeling empty. Like Mel and Kurt and Trent, he desperately wanted to find something that brought him satisfaction.

Maybe you're beginning a similar quest yourself. Most people do, especially when they're young. One thing these searches all have in common is that they contain the word *if*.

"I would be happy *if*..."

"I could be satisfied *if*..."

"I could get past this emptiness and depression *if*..."

The list of things people assume will fill the holes in their lives is long and wildly varied, but here are a few of the most common:

"I would be happy *if*...

- I had a boyfriend or girlfriend."

- I could have sex."

- I could have lots of fantastic sex."

- I could be free from my parents."

- I could have a close and loving family."

- I could get married and have kids."

- I could get my parents to love me."

- I could get my parents to love each other."

- I had enough money to be comfortable."

- I had enough money to get everything I want."

- I could get into the college I want."

- I were smarter."

- I were faster, stronger, and more athletic."

- I were popular."

- I didn't care so much about what people think."

- I could do something really important with my life."

- I could help people in a meaningful way."

- I could make a difference in the world."

- I could be a great artist or singer or actor or magician."

- I could just relax and party all the time."

- I didn't have to worry about anything."

- I could experiment as much as I want with drugs, alcohol, or anything else."

- I could be with the people I love the most."

How many people do you know who are trying to find meaning or satisfaction in one or more of those areas? How many people do you know who are convinced that money, good grades, a boyfriend, sex, popularity, a future, or a good reputation will make their lives complete? How many people do you know who are looking for something worth living for?

Have you noticed the same searching attitude in your own life? I've noticed it in my life. If we're honest with ourselves, we'll admit we all have an empty space or a quiet ache that makes itself known when we're alone with our thoughts. You don't have to be the king of Israel or Mel Gibson to be aware of it.

The question is: What do we do about that aching emptiness?

THREE OPTIONS

Before we commit the rest of our lives to chasing down our *ifs,* one by one, to try them out, let's take a close look at the experiences of people who've already done that. Let's see what we can learn from satisfaction-seekers who managed to capture every *if* on their lists. Let's examine the conclusions of Mel Gibson, Kurt Cobain, Trent Reznor, and King Solomon.

Let's answer the question: What do you do when you discover that nothing in this life can bring you satisfaction? Based on the experiences of those we mentioned, we get three possible answers.

1 :: KEEP SEARCHING ANYWAY.

Trent Reznor lost hope in things outside of himself and started looking inward. After exploring every pleasure life has to offer (including things many of us would never think of doing), he gave up on finding answers in external experiences. Remember his words: "After I got everything I ever wanted, I was ****ing worse off than I was before." With the help of psychological therapy, he's exploring his own heart and mind and says, "I feel better about myself as a human being right now than I ever did."

Reznor is convinced there's no meaning in anything life can offer. He still rejects religion, but he's holding out hope that there are answers in his own soul—apart from God. It feels good to him to keep looking. Like many of us, he just can't accept that nothing in this life will ever satisfy. He'll keep on searching.

2 :: GIVE UP.

Kurt Cobain apparently decided he had come to the end of his search. Outside of himself. Inside of himself. Nothing worked.

Nothing could ease his depression or fill the lack of meaning in his life. His suicide note made it clear he couldn't find any excitement for his art or the things that used to bring him joy. All of his searching turned up nothing worth living for.

Bible teacher Steve Stockman says Cobain's life points directly to the message of Solomon: "I think Cobain is Ecclesiastes made flesh. He is the perfect conclusion to a life without God. Fame, wealth, or whatever the modern world can offer is meaningless without God. What a scream from the heart of heaven to the culture of the day. In between the lines of the newscast on that sad day in April '94, the words 'Meaningless, meaningless all is meaningless' echoed around the world. God speaks loud and clear in the heart of our culture."

According to Kurt Cobain and King Solomon, those who are paying attention and who are being honest with themselves can only come to one conclusion: Nothing in this life will ever take away your emptiness. You might as well stop looking.

Of course, that's not all Solomon said. We'll look deeper into his conclusions throughout the rest of this book. But in the matter of finding meaning in this life, he and Kurt Cobain were in agreement.

3 :: LOOK OUTSIDE OF THIS LIFE.

We've already seen that Mel Gibson came to the same conclusion as Kurt Cobain. And that conclusion almost brought him to the same end as Cobain. So what kept Mel Gibson from jumping out that window? He told Diane Sawyer he found an answer that changed everything for him. It wasn't in the world of things. It had nothing to do with money or power. And, it wasn't hiding in his own heart.

Gibson's answer lay beyond this world.

While talking about his most successful movie ever, *The Passion of the Christ*, Gibson said this about the subject of his film: "He was beaten for our iniquities. He was wounded for our transgressions. And by his wounds, we are healed. That's the point of the film. It's about faith, hope, love, and forgiveness. It's the reality for me. I believe that. I have to."

"Have to?" Diane Sawyer asked him.

"I have to," Gibson repeated. "For my own sake. So I can hope. So I can live."

After experiencing everything life has to offer, Mel Gibson decided there's no meaning on earth apart from Jesus Christ. He tried it all, and his answer inspired him to invest $25 million of his own money—not to mention his reputation in Hollywood and around the world—to make a risky movie about Jesus.

I met Gibson while I was speaking at the DC/LA conference in Washington, D.C., and he was promoting *The Passion of the Christ* to Christian audiences around the country. Well...maybe *met* isn't the right word. He slapped my hand as he walked by me on stage in an auditorium filled with several thousand Christian students. People were going crazy over him, calling friends on their cell phones and shouting, "Mel Gibson is standing right in front of me!"

When everyone finally calmed down so he could talk, Gibson looked over the crowd and said something amazing: "I wish I had been like you. I wish I had spent more time honoring God when I was younger." Think about those words. The man who had it all, who had tried it all, wishes he had spent his life differently.

"Remember your Creator in the days of your youth"
(Ecclesiastes 12:1).

This book isn't about Mel Gibson. I don't think he's necessarily a great role model or a great teacher. He's just a man we can learn something from before we set off on our own search for meaning.

It's also not about Kurt Cobain. Or Trent Reznor. It's about someone who had more than all three of them put together. More fame. More power. More money. More sex. (Way more sex.) More friends. More romance. More good deeds. More artistic achievement. More world-changing success.

And more to say about all of it.

Solomon, the poet-king, learned the truth about life on earth the hard way. Before continuing your own search for something to fill the nagging emptiness of life—and before deciding you're already a Christian, so why bother—why not find out what he learned when he conducted the greatest experiment the world has ever known?

It could change everything about the way you live the rest of your life.

HOW TO TALK TO UNBELIEVING FRIENDS ABOUT FEELING EMPTY

It's not always easy for Christians to talk to unbelievers about things that really matter to us. We're worried about offending them. We don't want to make things weird in the friendship. But if you really care about your friends, these are conversations worth having. And the book of Ecclesiastes gives us a great place to start.

1 :: ASK YOUR FRIENDS IF THEY'RE EVER SURPRISED WHEN THEY HEAR ABOUT SOMEONE WHO HAS IT ALL BEING DEPRESSED OR SUICIDAL.

Ask why they think really successful people get depressed. What's missing? What's the real answer to feelings of sadness, depression, and the sense that there must be more to life than what we're experiencing? Ask your friends what helps them when they experience those feelings.

2 :: TALK ABOUT *IF ONLYS*.

Ask your friends to talk about the things they thought would make them feel satisfied with life. Be honest about your own list of *if onlys*, whether it includes money, a relationship with a specific person, or some incredible experience. Talk about the idea of unlimited wishes and how much it would take to truly satisfy. Be ready to explain the perspective that there's no such thing as "enough" to take away the emptiness of life on our own. Point to people such as Mel Gibson, Kurt Cobain, Trent Reznor, and King Solomon as examples.

3 :: TALK ABOUT THE DIFFERENCE BETWEEN EARTHLY RELIGION AND LOOKING TO GOD FOR REAL ANSWERS.

For some people, religion is just another *if only*. "If only I could become good enough for God, then I'd find true meaning in life." Ask your friends what they think about that idea. Explain that you don't believe it and Christianity doesn't teach it. The Bible doesn't say meaning is found in being perfect, because we can't achieve perfection. Be prepared to explain your understanding of the difference between practicing a religion in an effort to reach God and finding hope in a loving God, who has already reached out to you.

OBSERVATION EXERCISES

1. Look around your own life. Do you know any people who have come to the same conclusions as Mel Gibson, Kurt Cobain, or Trent Reznor? They don't have to be rock stars or millionaires. Even students can decide there's no meaning in life or there's only meaning outside of themselves.

2. Pay attention to the media (books, magazines, web sites, TV shows, songs, movies) you consume for the next few weeks. Do you hear anyone else saying things that sound like Solomon? Anyone talking about the emptiness of life or the search to fill that emptiness? Who's saying it? What are they saying? Do you think they're speaking the truth?

3. Observe your own heart. If you could snap your fingers right now and have anything in the world you could imagine, what would you ask for? Money? Knowledge? Sex? Relationships? Harder question: What do you think having those things would do for you? Do you believe the result would be any different than it was for Mel Gibson, Kurt Cobain, or Trent Reznor? Why or why not?

I've always been a science fan. I love conducting experiments— and not just because of the cool goggles and Bunsen burners. (Who doesn't like fire?) Like most people, I want to see for myself what's true and what's not. I want to make discoveries and find out how the world works.

THE HARD
THE HARD WAY
WAY

When I was six, my friend Geoff and I spent our days in the fields conducting experiments with my chemistry set and his microscope. Together we discovered that dry grass burns better than green grass. Black ants don't like red ants. And you can dig a long way without reaching the center of the earth.

All that experimenting is what led to our trouble with the cats. At the time it seemed like a good idea. Geoff swore it was a scientific fact that cats always land on their feet. I played the skeptic. I said maybe cats land on their feet *most* of the time, but surely not *all* of the time. And the experiment was on.

Assembling the necessary equipment was easy. Large, grassy area? Check. Adequate supply of kittens? Check. (My family always had dozens of outdoor cats.) Volunteer to propel the cats into the air? Check.

Here's how the experiment worked: Geoff would select a kitten, examine it, and hand it to me. I would then rev up the kitty and send it sailing into the wild blue sky. Boy, those kittens could fly. And sure enough, when they came down, they landed on all fours. Sure, they looked a little dizzy after the experiment, but they walked away unharmed for the most part.

As the experiment progressed, I began to throw each kitten a little higher than the previous one. And I watched in amazement as they managed to get their landing gear down just before impact. *It must be a fact*, I thought. *Cats always land on their feet.*

With reckless abandon, I threw one final test subject into the air. But this one didn't land on her feet. The little, blue-eyed kitten hit the ground with a thud—right on her delicate back. She started crying and so did I.

The kitten was severely injured. Several of her bones were obviously broken. Her breathing grew ragged. Geoff and I sat in silence for the next hour until the kitten finally passed away.

The mama cat walked up and started licking her kitten's white fur. Then she looked at me as though she knew the kitten's death was my fault.

Instead of being happy that our experiment had dispelled a timeless myth about cats, I felt terrible. The experiment had done its job, but I had thoughtlessly destroyed a life to discover the truth. I had killed a little kitten!

Even though I was only six at the time, I've never forgotten watching that kitten suffer and die. We buried her in the backyard where we buried all of our pets when they died.

Later that day something strange happened. The mama cat approached me and rubbed against my leg. I sat down, and she climbed in my lap and licked my hand. I couldn't believe she would be nice to me after what I had done to her kitten. It felt almost as though she was forgiving me.

I learned three things from that painful memory:

1. *Even if an experiment helps us find the truth, it can cost way more than the truth is worth.* Knowing cats don't always land on their feet wasn't worth the price of that kitten's life. Sometimes it's better to learn the truth from someone who's already done the necessary experimenting. You don't have to learn every truth the hard way.

2. *Sometimes we can discover powerful truth about God just by observing the world he created.* I don't know if that mama cat was really forgiving me for killing her kitten, but her act of kindness became a powerful demonstration to me of how God could forgive me after his Son died on the cross for my sin.

3. *There's more to know about life than we can discover through experiments and observations alone. Ultimate truth can only be found through God.* You can learn a lot about kittens and ants and fire and people by paying attention to the world around you— and that information is valuable. But watching that kitten die didn't tell me why animals and people perish—or why God forgives those who trust in his Son. Finding the ultimate answers to questions about life and death requires something beyond what I can experience naturally. Those answers require wisdom from someone who can see past our lives "under the sun."

Just to be clear, even though I was six when this happened I am not pleased with my actions. I am a cat lover and have rescued cats from shelters, including the one that now lives with my family, Isabella.

LOOKING AND ASKING

Every experiment starts with an observation or question. Do cats land on all fours all of the time? Do heavy objects fall faster than light objects? What happens when you split an atom? How many licks does it take to get to the Tootsie Roll® center of a Tootsie Pop®?

All of those questions led to experiments that led to answers that helped us figure out more about how life works. Finding such answers usually starts with making observations about life, then asking questions based on those observations. This book deals with one of the greatest experiments of all time. And that experiment started when a wise man looked at his life and the world around him and asked one of the greatest questions of all time.

Solomon, king of Israel, recorded the process and results of his experiment in the biblical book of Ecclesiastes. Solomon had the guts to ask the hardest question this life presents. Unlike anyone who lived before or since (including Mel Gibson), Solomon had the ability to gather the necessary equipment to conduct an effective experiment to answer the question. Alone, among all the people of the earth, Solomon had the God-given wisdom to interpret the results of his experiment.

Before we get into the experiment itself, let's take a closer look at the experimenter. Ecclesiastes 1:1 begins with this introduction:

> The words of the Teacher, son of David, king in Jerusalem.

Solomon never identifies himself by name in the book. As a result, some scholars suggest he didn't write Ecclesiastes. But the oldest traditions and the book's own evidence point directly to the poet-king. For starters, the writer acknowledges he is King David's son and is himself the king of Israel. He drops enough clues about his wisdom and wealth later in the book to confirm his ID. But instead of giving us his name, he calls himself a term that's translated as "Teacher."

The term comes from the Hebrew word *Koheleth*. Bible scholars debate the ultimate meaning of the word Solomon chose for his name tag ("Hi, I'm *Koheleth*. I'll be conducting this experiment"). The root of the word means "to assemble, compile, or gather." So some Bible translations use the word *preacher* or *teacher,* meaning "one who assembles the people to teach them something (or one who teaches in the assembly)." Others think the word means "one who gathers and compiles great writings or books," as Solomon also did.

The meaning I like best for the word *Koheleth* is "one who gathers information for the purpose of finding the truth." Another way to say it would be to call him a "searcher." Solomon identifies himself as the searching one, the one who hunts for something valuable.

What was he searching for? The answer to his big question. What was his big question? You'll find it in the poem he wrote in Ecclesiastes 1:2-11. By examining his words, we can see what observations drove Solomon to conduct his groundbreaking experiment.

As we mentioned in chapter 1, Solomon was a guy who had it all. As with Mel Gibson, Kurt Cobain, Trent Reznor, and so many others, his observations weren't very positive.

> [2]"Meaningless! Meaningless!"
> says the Teacher.
> "Utterly meaningless!
> Everything is meaningless."

Then he begins to describe why he feels so despairing about life on earth.

> [3]What does man gain from all his labor
> at which he toils under the sun?
> [4]Generations come and generations go,
> but the earth remains forever.

First, he notices that while nature seems to keep going and going, the most sophisticated thing in nature—humans—live very briefly before being replaced by the next generation.

> [5]The sun rises and the sun sets,
> and hurries back to where it rises.
> [6]The wind blows to the south
> and turns to the north;
> round and round it goes,
> ever returning on its course.

For a guy who was writing almost a thousand years before Jesus was born, Solomon's observations were pretty advanced. His descriptions of wind patterns seem to capture the idea of what meteorologists now call the jet stream, a concept modern scientists didn't identify until a few hundred years ago.

> [7]All streams flow into the sea,
> yet the sea is never full.
> To the place the streams come from,
> there they return again.

In the same way, he describes the cycle water travels on the earth. Remember drawing pictures of the water cycle in grade school? Water in streams and rivers flows into bigger rivers, which eventually flow into the ocean. Then instead of filling up the ocean, some of the water evaporates into the atmosphere, where it forms rain clouds. The rains run off into streams and rivers and start the whole cycle again.

Solomon saw it happening long before scientists understood why it happened. He saw that God's creation has the amazing ability to renew itself, to keep going, to regenerate season after season. In short he saw that nature is endless, but human life on this earth is temporary.

[8]All things are wearisome,
more than one can say.
The eye never has enough of seeing,
nor the ear its fill of hearing.
[9]What has been will be again,
what has been done will be done again;
there is nothing new under the sun.

Instead of being excited by all the amazing things he saw in nature, Solomon found them depressing. Not just the recycling of nature, but the fact that humans can never get enough of it. No matter how much we see, hear, or learn, we can't be satisfied.

[10]Is there anything of which one can say,
"Look! This is something new"?
It was here already, long ago;
it was here before our time.

As we'll see in the next chapter, Solomon was a writer, artist, and inventor. The fact that he would never discover or create anything truly new depressed him. As did the fact that everything seems to keep going the way it always has.

[11]There is no remembrance of men of old,
and even those who are yet to come
will not be remembered
by those who follow.

Solomon also recognized being a superstar in your own time wasn't worth very much, because everyone is eventually forgotten. Life is short, and when you're gone from this earth, you're gone forever.

IDENTIFYING THE QUESTION

Solomon was depressed about his observations of life on this planet. His experiment wasn't just something he was kind of curious about. It wasn't just a random idea he decided to test. His observations of life led him to a question that really messed up his mind and his mood.

Instead of being excited about the advanced scientific observations he was making, Solomon saw them as evidence of a problem for humans—namely, nothing ever changes. No matter what anyone does, the world keeps going on and on and on. Therefore, one person can't make any real difference in the world. Even millions of people can't make a real difference on a planet where nothing ever changes.

To put it another way: Life is meaningless. No one can ever see enough or hear enough to be truly satisfied. No matter what happens, eventually your life ends, and other people take your place. Nature just keeps going.

So we come to the question: What's the point of it all? Where's the meaning in life?

Maybe you've wondered the same thing. Lots of people do, especially students. You recognize you could work your whole life to be rich, successful, and happy. But you ask, what's the point if you just end up dead like everyone else?

Mel Gibson wondered that. So did Kurt Cobain and Trent Reznor. And they're not alone. The hugely successful rock band U2 wrote a song called, "I Still Haven't Found What I'm Looking For," in spite of their riches, adventures, and religious experiences.

Pink Floyd recorded the classic album *The Wall,* which is the story of a guy who dreams of becoming a rock star and eventually makes his dream come true. In the end though, he discovers that his fame, fortune, and art can't make him happy. None of it gives him any meaning in life. He concludes that everything is just "another brick in the wall."

As we'll see in the next chapter, King Solomon lived a life that put rock stars to shame. He had more wealth, power, sex, achievement, fame, knowledge, and even love than anyone could dream of. Still he was left with one impression: "Utterly meaningless! Everything is meaningless."

If a guy like Solomon thought life was meaningless, what hope do any of us have of finding meaning in our own lives on earth? If you can be that rich, that powerful, that famous, that artistic—and still not be happy—why go on? What's the point of trying? Of working? Of hoping? That's what Solomon wanted to know. And that's where the experiment comes in.

THE GREAT EXPERIMENT

Instead of giving up, Solomon the Searcher hatched a plan. He would conduct an experiment to search the world of pleasure to find something that brings meaning to life, something to make life worth living.

Check out what he wrote in Ecclesiastes 1:12-13: "I, the Teacher, was king over Israel in Jerusalem. I devoted myself to study and to explore by wisdom all that is done under heaven."

Notice that Solomon conducted his experiment on everything "under heaven." He wanted to make absolutely sure there was nothing he could do on this side of heaven to fill the empty places in his heart.

His plan was to use his great wealth and wisdom to test every experience in life. The book of Ecclesiastes records each phase of his experiment. Imagine his anticipation! Would he find meaning in knowledge and wisdom? Would he find it in pleasure? In riches? Accomplishments? Long life? Love? Sex? Romance? Power? Would he find meaning in anything?

Solomon wasn't hopeful. "What a heavy burden God has laid on men! I have seen all the things that are done under the sun; all of them are meaningless, a chasing after the wind" (Ecclesiastes 1:13-14).

That was Solomon's take on life. And before you read much further, you need to determine whether his opinion is trustworthy. Why should you listen to Solomon? What qualifies him to conduct this experiment? What gives him the right to come up with the final answers?

In the next chapter, we're going to hold a magnifying glass up to Solomon's life—just to make sure he's worth listening to. The stakes are too high to trust these questions and answers to just anyone.

But if Solomon does turn out to be a qualified judge, think of how valuable his answers would be. They'd be priceless. Many people spend their whole lives running similar experiments on their own—trying out each of their *ifs* in search of anything that satisfies, anything that might give their lives meaning.

Sex. Drugs. Money. Marriage after marriage. Religion. Endless varieties of relationships. Exercise and a perfect body. Entertainment. People will throw themselves into anything that might give them the satisfaction they crave.

Why shouldn't they, you might ask. Why shouldn't people find out for themselves what will make them happy in life?

The answer goes back to the kitten I killed. Remember how I foolishly destroyed that life in order to find the answer to my experiment? How much worse would it be to destroy your own life looking for an answer Solomon already discovered? Why waste the next 50 years of your life looking for meaning in all the wrong places if you can find it right in the pages of Solomon's book? Why end up wishing you'd honored God when you were young, instead of conducting your own experiment?

HOW TO TALK TO UNBELIEVING FRIENDS ABOUT THE SEARCH FOR MEANING IN LIFE

Talking to unbelieving friends and family about things such as God and faith can sometimes feel awkward. The book of Ecclesiastes can help you kick off some great conversations, because Solomon starts with things everyone can observe.

1 :: ASK YOUR FRIENDS IF THEY'VE EVER CONDUCTED ANY EXPERIMENTS ON THEIR OWN.

Be ready to tell your own stories of experiments you've conducted. Ask whether your friends' experiments helped them find answers—or just led to more questions. If they could do an experiment to find just one truth in the universe, what would it be? Why? What would it be worth to them to discover that truth? Have them think in terms of time, money, and sacrifice. How much would be too much to sacrifice to discover that truth?

2 :: ASK YOUR FRIENDS IF THEY'VE EVER SUSPECTED THAT EVERYTHING IN LIFE IS MEANINGLESS.

Again when you ask questions such as this in a serious conversation, be ready to answer them yourself. What do your friends think brings ultimate meaning to life? How do they know? Is there any way to find out? What do you think?

3 :: ASK WHAT YOUR FRIENDS' OBSERVATIONS TELL THEM ABOUT THE WORLD.

Solomon learned a lot by just paying attention to the world around him. Have your friends or family seen things that convinced them there's meaning to be found in life? Have they seen things that have convinced them to give up looking for meaning in some areas? What have they noticed in life that really matters? What have you noticed?

4 :: ASK YOUR FRIENDS WHO THEY TRUST TO ANSWER LIFE'S BIGGEST QUESTIONS.

Obviously we can't observe everything in life for ourselves, so we learn to trust others to give us information about important issues. For example, we trust the people who went to the moon to tell us what it's like. We trust reporters and soldiers to describe the experience of battle to us. Who do your friends and family trust to describe observations about big subjects such as the meaning of life, the existence of God, and the reality of heaven and hell? Can they trust anyone? Who do you trust? Why?

OBSERVATION EXERCISES

1. Whether they realize it or not, people test ideas and approaches to life all the time. Look around at the people in your school, church, and family. Do you notice anyone who seems to be testing something? Perhaps some are trying to discover what impact new clothes or a new hairstyle will have on themselves or others. Perhaps some are testing people in authority to find the limits of what they can get away with. Perhaps others are experimenting with how little studying they can do and still get a passing grade. What do you notice?

2. Make a short list of things you learned about your world today simply by observing what's going on around you. For example, if you observe the refrigerator is almost empty, you might conclude your parents haven't had time to buy groceries in a while. Or if you notice someone is sunburned, you can guess they've spent a lot of time outside lately. Jot down a handful of such observations from your own life as well as what you can learn from them.

3. Think about some of the smartest people you know. In general do they seem happy, content, and satisfied with life? Now ask yourself the same question about people you know who are rich, popular, or "good Christians"? Does any one group seem happier or more satisfied with life than the others? Why do you

think that is? Where does a sense of contentment and satisfaction come from?

4. Observe your own heart. Do you ever experience the emotions Solomon described? Do you ever feel an emptiness or groaning in your heart that doesn't seem to go away completely, no matter what you do? Do you ever feel as though life might be meaningless? Why do you think that is?

WHAT SOLOMON

WHAT SOLOMON HAD THAT YOU DON'T

HAD THAT YOU DON'T

Have you ever participated in a taste test? You know, where you try different brands of orange juice or yogurt or microwavable bacon and talk about which one you like better?

If you've never done it before, here's how it works. Let's say you're testing soda. The tester fills two paper cups—one with, say, Pepsi° and the other with Coke°—and sets them in front of a cardboard barrier. You take a drink of one, then the other, and pick your favorite. The tester then removes the barrier to show you which one you picked. Fair and square.

But what if the test wasn't fair and square? What would you think of someone who declared over and over that Pepsi° was the best cola in the world—without ever having tried Coke°? What kind of test would it be if someone drank from only one of the cups? How can someone be qualified to say what's best if he's never tried the alternatives? That would be fraud, declaring an answer before you have all the information.

Several years ago I noticed many students were e-mailing me about my opinion of different movies.

So I started a Web site called www.planetwisdom.com. My goal was to create a place where students could discuss movies from a Christian perspective.

Those of us who write reviews for the site have joked that some movies are so predictable we could write reviews of them without ever actually seeing them. But actually doing that would be a lie, wouldn't it? A person who hasn't seen a movie isn't qualified to tell you how good or bad that movie is.

So for an experiment or an opinion to be valid, the tester has to have a complete body of information. He must test all available alternatives. Therefore, before we trust Solomon to tell us if anything in life brings real meaning or lasting satisfaction, we'd better make sure he was able to test everything worth testing.

While we're at it, we should also test Solomon's credentials to make sure he's really qualified to understand and explain the results of his experiment. Otherwise, he's just another guy with an opinion. And what good would that do us? Think about it. We don't really want to hear what the guys from *Dumb and Dumber* think about the meaning of life. Although it might be funny to watch Lloyd and Harry test everything "under the sun," their conclusions wouldn't be very valuable to us. No, if we're going to trust the results of Solomon's experiment, we've got to know he's a qualified judge.

In making that call, we have to ask: How could any one person possibly have the opportunity to try all the alternatives in life—and be qualified to deliver trustworthy answers about his findings? Very few people in history would even come close to being qualified to run that kind of experiment.

Now don't get me wrong. All of us can observe life and come up with certain ideas about what matters and what doesn't. We've already seen, in fact, that many people have reached some of the same conclusions Solomon did on their own. And as we study the book of Ecclesiastes, many of us will agree with him based on our own experiences. But we're looking for the most qualified guy who ever lived to confirm our suspicions about life once and for all. We want to find bottom-line truth—not just more questions.

Solomon might be the only person who ever lived who had the credentials to do the job right. He met both requirements—the unique ability to judge whether anything brought meaning to life and endless opportunities to try it all. Let's start with the first qualification as we get to know our experimenter a little better.

THE WISDOM OF SOLOMON

Solomon had giant shoes to fill. He grew up knowing that his dad, King David, was the greatest ruler in Israel's history. David was famous throughout the land as a warrior, an adventurer, a great leader, a poet, and a man who had a very close relationship with God.

Solomon's dad was the guy who killed Goliath the giant with a slingshot when he was probably just a teenager. He was the guy who had conquered all of Israel's enemies and made the small country unbelievably wealthy. God himself called David a man after his own heart (see Acts 13:22).

Solomon probably didn't grow up expecting to succeed his father as king of Israel. He had older brothers who were more likely candidates. But when David was very close to the end of his life, his favorite wife Bathsheba and God's prophet Nathan requested that David name Solomon king, in spite of the fact that David's priest and the head of his army were backing an older son. In fact they'd already begun a celebration of the older son's kingship.

But David settled on Solomon and turned the rule of the kingdom over to the young man. Imagine the pressure Solomon must have felt. Not only did he have to follow a legend, but the nation was struggling to hold itself together in the wake of David's death. Several powerful national leaders had supported Solomon's older, better-known brother. And after 40 years of following the same king, everyone was watching to see how young Solomon would lead the people.

Yikes! Talk about pressure! Solomon wanted to be a good king, but he was unsure of himself. Who wouldn't be?

Shortly after he became king, Solomon made a huge sacrifice of animals to God to show his love for the Lord. In spite of the fact that Solomon had already made a couple of mistakes, God responded to his sincere heart by doing something very unusual. He appeared to Solomon personally in a dream. God himself appeared, not an angel or a prophet. Then God did something even rarer. He told Solomon, "Ask for whatever you want me to give you" (1 Kings 3:5).

Now God is no genie in a bottle. He loves to give his children good gifts, but we don't know of anyone else but Solomon who was presented with a blank check and told "fill in whatever you want." Imagine if you were in that position—God standing ready to deliver anything you could dream up in the entire universe. What would you go for?

Maybe the first thing that comes to mind is money—enough to make Bill Gates jealous. Or fame. Or absolute power over everyone. Or endless health. Or perfect relationships. Or perhaps you'd go for supernatural abilities such as flying or being invisible or reading people's minds. It's a little scary even to think about how we would respond if God gave us the same opportunity he gave Solomon.

What did Solomon ask for? Remember, he had just inherited the highest-stress job in the world. So he said:

> Now, O Lord my God, you have made your servant king in place of my father David. But I am only a little child and do not know how to carry out my duties. Your servant is here among the people you have chosen, a great people, too numerous to count or number. So give your servant a discerning heart to govern your people and to distinguish between right and wrong (1 Kings 3:7-9).

Solomon asked for wisdom to lead the people of Israel and discernment to know right from wrong. God liked that request. He appreciated Solomon's unselfishness and humility. And he delivered what Solomon asked for—by the truckload. Check out God's answer: "I will do what you have asked. I will give you a wise and discerning heart, so that there will never have been anyone like you, nor will there ever be" (1 Kings 3:12).

In other words God made Solomon the wisest human being who ever lived. Period. God said it, so we can trust that no one else was ever as wise as Solomon. How's that for being qualified to run a test about the meaning of life?

Everyone who knew Solomon was blown away by his wisdom. People saw it in his conversation, in his decisions regarding the kingdom, and in his writings. He became world famous as the wisest man on earth. Here's what 1 Kings 4:29-34 says about him:

> God gave Solomon wisdom and very great insight, and a breadth of understanding as measureless as the sand on the seashore. Solomon's wisdom was greater than the wisdom of all the men of the East, and greater than all the wisdom of Egypt. He was wiser than any other man.... And his fame spread to all the surrounding nations. He

spoke three thousand proverbs and his songs numbered a thousand and five. He described plant life, from the cedar of Lebanon to the hyssop that grows out of walls. He also taught about animals and birds, reptiles and fish. Men of all nations came to listen to Solomon's wisdom, sent by all the kings of the world, who had heard of his wisdom.

Solomon's wisdom wasn't just spiritual and religious. If you're picturing an old guy with a long beard on top of a mountain saying profound and confusing things about God, you've got the wrong image. Solomon was a relatively young guy, and his wisdom was practical. He applied it to real-life stuff such as relationships, money, emotions, work, pleasure, and time management.

Solomon was also a scientist who studied and taught about plants and animals and weather patterns. He had the supernatural ability from God to observe life and come to the right conclusions about it. Nobody else in all of history was as qualified as Solomon to conduct a test such as the one described in Ecclesiastes. Nobody.

But what about the test itself? Did Solomon really have the capability to test everything "under the sun" for meaning and life-fulfilling purpose?

ENDLESS OPPORTUNITIES

The ideal person to conduct the experiment would have needed so much money that he wouldn't hesitate to spend a fortune trying something that may or may not pay off. He also would have needed decades of free time, which means he'd have to have lots of people available to take care of things for him. He would have needed access to every kind of pleasure or entertainment anyone could dream up. And he'd have to be powerful enough to accomplish any goal he set for himself.

We've just described Solomon's life.

As the king of Israel, Solomon had absolute power. If a law dictated against something he wanted to try, he could just change the law. Nobody could stop him. If what he set his heart on required a lot of time, he had the power to set everything else aside and concentrate on that one thing for as long as it took to thoroughly test it.

Money was certainly not a problem. Solomon inherited a multi-billion dollar kingdom from his dad, King David. And with Solomon's business sense and the government's heavy taxation on the people, he increased the size of the kingdom tremendously.

As for love, romance, and sex, we're told Solomon loved many, many women. And many women loved him. His Song of Songs, the book that follows Ecclesiastes in your Bible, may be one of the greatest romantic love poems of all time. Full of beautiful imagery, the book describes a sexually intimate love story between a man and a woman. Solomon himself thoroughly tested the pleasures of sex. With 700 wives and 300 concubines, it's safe to say he had a reputation as a sexual adventurer.

As for achievement and success, Solomon had the chance to test those boundaries, as well. We've already seen that he wrote thousands of proverbs, poems, and books. He also built God's spectacular temple, one of the seven wonders of the ancient world. Not to mention his own palace, which was even larger than the temple. Solomon definitely made his mark.

On top of all of that, he had endless opportunities to indulge himself in all the entertainment, music, drinking, eating, and laughter his heart desired. Solomon literally had no limits on his life. He wasn't like us. He didn't have to settle for less than his heart desired.

Last year, I became obsessed with a grill that was on sale at a local store. Imagine 836 square inches of grilling space with a burner dedicated for pots and pans and a smoker box. (Did I mention I love to cook?) This baby was big and beautiful, and I couldn't stop thinking about all the stuff I could grill on it, including my homemade pizzas. The only problem was that the grill cost $988.

I probably could have come up with the money one way or another, but there were just too many other things to spend it on. I couldn't justify the cost. So, in a sense, I had to give up exploring that grill to see what level of satisfaction it would bring me.

Sometimes the limitation isn't money. When the *Spiderman 2* video game came out, I hit the video game store at the mall to check it out. *Wow.* I loved it. Especially the way you can swing through the whole city with Spidey. Very cool. And I could have come up with the $50, but I realized I didn't have the time to sit in front of my TV and play the game to find out what kind of meaning it would bring to my life. I was limited by all the other things I had to do.

One more example. On the Fourth of July last year, I was visiting my family in California. And I had the urge to blow stuff up and send stuff flying. Unfortunately California has these incredibly restrictive laws about fireworks (probably because of all the wildfires they've had). All I could do was light off a few sparklers in a very limited area. Back home in Texas, I could have been lighting off sticks of dynamite in the back yard (okay, not really—but close). But in California the law prevented me from exploring what my heart desired.

I've got hundreds of examples like this. You do too. Some of them involve good things we long for, but we just can't get. And we're left to wonder if those things would really make our lives full and satisfying. Others concern things we desire to explore that aren't as healthy—sex outside of marriage, drugs, wrong relationships—things we know would hurt us in the end. But we still wonder if we're missing out on something big, because we haven't tried them.

Solomon tried it all—the good, the bad, and the ugly. "I denied myself nothing my eyes desired" (Ecclesiastes 2:10). Solomon had unlimited opportunities to test everything the human heart might dream up to see if it really pays off the way we hope it will. Everything.

In the next few chapters, we'll explore each phase of the experiment and look at why Solomon kept reporting that "Everything is meaningless!"

Let the experiment begin!

HOW TO TALK TO UNBELIEVING FRIENDS ABOUT WISDOM AND EXPERIENCE

Unbelievers and even some Christians make the mistake of thinking everyone in the Bible is some kind of perfect, goody-goody saint who never did anything wrong. Or they assume every word in the Bible was written by people who never experienced "the real world." Solomon was not that guy.

1 :: ASK YOUR FRIENDS HOW MUCH ANY ONE PERSON CAN REALLY EXPERIENCE IN ONE LIFETIME.

This builds on an important discussion point from the last chapter. Can any one person experience everything there is to experience in one lifetime? If not, how can anyone know for sure he or she is not missing out on life's key ingredient for meaning? You might mention that Solomon came about as close as anyone to doing it all. Ask your friends if they rely only on what they can experience firsthand in life or if they've realized they're going to have to trust others' input in order to make decisions about what really matters in life.

2 :: ASK YOUR FRIENDS HOW THEY DECIDE WHO THEY WILL TRUST FOR VITAL INFORMATION.

As Christians we're used to the idea of taking the Bible as the final standard on what's true and what isn't. Unbelievers don't necessarily accept that standard, but as we saw in the first question, they have to trust someone eventually. Ask how they decide who is trustworthy. Do they ever accept another source's word as final—or do they just go through life thinking you can't really know anything for sure? Be ready to explain why you've decided the Bible is a trustworthy source of truth.

3 :: ASK YOUR FRIENDS IF THEY KNOW ANYONE WHO SEEMS TO HAVE A LOT OF WISDOM AND A LOT OF EXPERIENCE.

Start out by explaining why you think Solomon's combination of wisdom and experience was unique. Mention that he is known not only as someone from the Bible, but also as a historical figure. The descriptions of his life in the Bible are consistent with what we know from history about kings of that era. Ask about the people in their lives who have a good combination of life experience and wisdom—the ability to really understand life. Do you know anyone like that? Are those people a trustworthy source of information? If Solomon fit that pattern, would he be trustworthy?

OBSERVATION EXERCISES

1. Write down the names of three people you know personally, whom you trust most to give you wisdom, direction, and right answers. Why do you trust those people? What is it about them that's convinced you to rely on them? Now jot down the names of three people you would not trust for wisdom, direction, or truth. Why are they on your list? What's the difference between those people and the first three you listed?

2. Pay attention to the news and entertainment media this week. Who are a few people being discussed who have a wide range of experiences in life, people who have tried many things life has to offer? Would you consider any of them wise? Why or why not? Have you noticed any truly wise people making the news lately? Does wisdom—not just knowledge—seem to be valued in the media? Why do you think that is?

3. Notice the people in your life this week. What do they seem to rely on most for direction in life? Their own experiences and insights? Parents and teachers? Their friends? Media figures? Who do these people seem to be following, and where are they being lead? Do you think they're aware of who they're following?

4. Observe your own heart. If you had your whole life to dedicate to conducting Solomon's search, could you ever experience as much as he did? Would you ever have as much wisdom to come up with the right answers? Do you think the Bible and Solomon's writings in it are trustworthy? If so, are you ready to take his answers as truth?

SOLOMON'S

SOLOMON'S PARTY PALACE

PARTY PALACE

At some point between the ages of eight and eighteen, the word *party* changes meaning for many of us. When you're a little kid, partying is all about pointy cardboard hats, colorful balloons, a big cake, maybe a clown. But for high school students and especially college students, the word means something else completely. When the guys in the dorm say, "Let's party," no one expects cake.

On many college campuses during the school year, the weekend starts on Thursday night with a bash that includes all the usual stuff; lots of alcohol, loud music, fun-seekers of both genders, people laughing and relaxing, maybe some drugs. Let's be honest, that kind of partying offers a pretty good time. It's full of things that bring pleasure.

Solomon knew how to party. In his experiment to see if anything in life can bring real meaning, lasting satisfaction, or inner peace, one of the first things he mentions is pleasure. And he's not talking just about sex. (We'll explore his experiences with sex and romance in the next chapter.) Pleasure includes all kinds of things that feel good.

Here's how Solomon put it in Ecclesiastes 2:1-3, 8, 10:

> I thought in my heart, "Come now, I will test you with pleasure to find out what is good." But that also proved to be meaningless. "Laughter," I said, "is foolish. And what does pleasure accomplish?" I tried cheering myself with wine, and embracing folly—my mind still guiding me with wisdom. I wanted to see what was worthwhile for men to do under heaven during the few days of their lives.
>
> I acquired men and women singers, and a harem as well—the delights of the heart of man…. I denied myself nothing my eyes desired; I refused my heart no pleasure.

It made sense for Solomon to dig into the world of pleasure to see if any of it made him happy. For one thing he had an all-access pass to every kind of pleasure he could dream up. But there's more to it than that. If you suspect life is really meaningless, pleasure is a great escape, isn't it? Laughter. Drinking. Acting goofy. Music. Dancing. Sex. Not holding back. Giving yourself permission to do what your body *really* wants to do. What a great way to forget about feeling empty!

The hard-core partiers I knew in college would have added an "Amen!" to that. These were guys who'd been given sudden freedom, away from their parents, to try out every pleasure they could get their hands on. They were also facing a scary time in their lives—wondering what the future held for them and still not sure what the world was all about. Their reaction to that fear and uncertainty could be summed up in two words: "Let's party!"

That's the partying motto: "If time is a waste of life, and life is a waste of time, then let's get wasted and have the time of our lives!"

Solomon considered that philosophy and said, "I'll give it a shot."

Before we explore the outcome of Solomon's quest to live for pleasure, let's make it clear that not all pleasure is bad. God created humans to experience pleasure. That's why laughing feels so good. And why music can have such a powerful effect on your mood.

Sitting in a comfortable chair. Hanging out with friends. Dancing. Feeling a cool breeze on a hot day. God gives us all kinds of pleasures to enjoy.

Solomon, however, took his quest for pleasure to the next level. He said to his heart, "Let's see if living for pleasure really satisfies." There's a huge difference between enjoying life's pleasures as a gift from God and making pleasure the whole point of your life.

Living for pleasure is called hedonism. Hedonists abide by the phrase, "If it feels good, do it." They worship pleasure. For them feeling good is the point of life. So you might say Solomon became a hedonist.

LAUGHING IT UP

The king started his quest for pleasure with laughter. Who doesn't like to laugh, especially with a group of friends? Solomon could afford to hire the finest comedians and joke writers in the world to come and entertain him.

Imagine being able to hire the people on TV and in movies who really crack you up and get them to put on shows for you every day. Will Ferrell. Chris Rock. Adam Sandler. Jim Carrey. All of them hanging out with you 24-7 just to make you and your friends laugh.

When it came to friends, Solomon had plenty to spare. His palace was crowded with wives, friends, family, servants, little kids, and lots of women. That joint must have rocked with laughter while Solomon was testing this area of pleasure.

And laughter *is* pleasure. I love to laugh with my family and friends. Even better, I love to make other people laugh. It's addictive to stand in front of an auditorium full of people and make them crack up. One time I walked right off the front of the stage while speaking at a summer camp. I fell about five feet and didn't even know what had happened. As I lay on my back in pain, all I could hear was the uproarious laughter of several hundred teenagers. I'm glad they had such a good time. Sometimes they laugh with you and sometimes they laugh at you.

With his wit and his wisdom, I'll bet Solomon could get his party people rolling in the aisles. That must have been a real high.

Someone once called laughter an instant vacation. And did you know it's good for you? Doctors tell us laughing strengthens the immune system. Clinical research has revealed laughing can help people with diabetes control their blood sugar after eating.

An organization called The Laughing Lab took laughter so seriously that it conducted the most extensive survey ever to find out what more than 100,000 people thought was the funniest joke in the world. Here's the one rated highest of those the lab tested:

> Sherlock Holmes and Dr. Watson are on a camping trip. They pitch their tent under the stars and go to sleep. Sometime in the middle of the night, Holmes wakes Watson up and says, "Watson, look up at the stars and tell me what you deduce."

Watson says, "I see millions of stars, and even if a few of those have planets, it's quite likely there are some planets like earth. And if there are a few planets like earth out there, there might also be life."

Holmes replied, "Watson, you idiot, somebody stole our tent."

Whether that joke made you laugh or not, you know you wanted to. We all want to laugh sometimes. That's why Americans watch hundreds, even thousands, of hours of TV sitcoms every year. That's why *The Simpsons, Seinfeld*, and all those other reruns seem to be on around the clock. We're all looking for something to make us cut loose and roar with laughter.

But if laughter is so effective, why does Solomon almost immediately say "Laughter is foolish"? He tried it on as a lifestyle. He enjoyed it. But when the laughter stopped, he found himself in the exact same place he was before it started. The laughter didn't solve any of his problems or bring meaning to his life. He discovered even something as good as laughter can't possibly fill a person's emptiness.

I grew up in Southern California. Some of my good friends tried to make it as stand-up comedians. At night I'd go with them to comedy clubs to watch them perform. After a while it became obvious that at some of the clubs, the only people who showed up were regulars. Every night they came to the club looking for some relief from their lives through laughter and drinking.

The thing was most of them didn't look very happy. After having seen so many comedians, they didn't laugh very easily. They'd get off work every night, drive to the club, sit around and drink, and wait for a few chuckles, then drive home. What an empty life they had trying to find a little meaning in laughter!

Have you ever heard little kids keep laughing at a joke long after everyone else has stopped? They want to prolong the moment by continuing to act goofy. If you've ever had that experience, you know how annoying it is to hear someone laugh for no reason—especially when it's time to be serious.

That's why Solomon wrote in Ecclesiastes 7:6: "Like the crackling of thorns under the pot, so is the laughter of fools. This too is meaningless." When something isn't funny anymore, you can't keep laughing (or faking laughter) to try to get that feeling back. Laughter just can't keep satisfying you.

WINE AND MUSIC

After his experiment with laughter failed, Solomon turned to other forms of pleasure, starting with wine. As the wealthy king of Israel, he probably had access to the finest wines from around the world. And his wine cellar never ran dry. He would have been able to test endlessly the effects of wine on his mood, his emotions, and his relationships.

If laughter is an instant vacation, wine and other alcohol offer much longer ones. Alcohol and drugs alter the way we see the world and the way our bodies react to things. In fact, booze can make you a whole new person—though not necessarily a better one.

But that's not something most people think about when they indulge in alcohol and drugs. All they care about is the pleasure that comes from getting drunk or getting high. They want to escape the stresses of everyday life by putting themselves in a state of mind where they don't care as much. Hard-core partiers claim drinking makes life more bearable for them. At least until they wake up the next morning.

Solomon's party palace flowed with great wine. He explored all that alcohol could offer him. Instead of being wise in his use of wine, he purposefully acted like a fool. In Ecclesiastes 2:3, he admits to "embracing folly." One definition of *folly* that I love is "instant gratification." A fool is someone who doesn't think about the consequences of his actions before he does something.

Keep in mind, though, that Solomon was still being guided by his supernatural wisdom from God (Ecclesiastes 2:3). He still had what he needed to come up with the right conclusions about his test. But that didn't keep him from experiencing all wine and folly had to offer. His conclusion: Meaningless. Wine gave him only temporary relief—and left him with nothing but emptiness.

Later in the passage, Solomon describes experimenting with music in his quest for meaning in life. At that time in history, musicians needed a rich sponsor to pay them to write and perform their music. Solomon "owned" the best singers his money could buy. Imagine being able to order all your favorite artists to perform your favorite songs any time you wanted.

"According to your request, king, tonight we'll be hearing Eminem, followed by Avril, Usher, and then a long set from Metallica." Not the bands you'd hire? How about having Mercy Me, Jeremy Camp, and Third Day lead you and your friends in a time of worship every night? Or make your own playlist—a different one for every day of the week.

Actually, in the mp3 era, we come close to having that kind of freedom and power. I love music, and my mp3 player is one of my best friends. It might be the best invention of my lifetime. At this moment, I have 1,661 songs loaded and ready to perform for me at any moment I feel the need for the energy, emotion, and good feelings music gives me. For me that's real pleasure.

Still as Solomon said, it's just a temporary relief for hearts that long for real and lasting meaning. As always he concluded, "Everything was meaningless, a chasing after the wind; nothing was gained under the sun" (Ecclesiastes 2:11).

THE HIGH COST OF LIVING FOR PLEASURE

It's important to say this again: Pleasure is not evil by itself. Paul wrote to Timothy that God "richly provides us with everything for our enjoyment" (1 Timothy 6:17). Enjoying the pleasure that comes from God's good gifts of laughter, music, sex as part of marriage, and all the rest of life is good. It's right. It's healthy.

So why not live for pleasure then? Why not indulge and let yourself go? Pleasure lovers don't understand why some of us resist, why we stay home from certain parties or keep ourselves away from the harmful side of pleasure. They might even make fun of us. "They think it strange that you do not plunge with them into the same flood of dissipation, and they heap abuse on you" (1 Peter 4:4).

But living as Solomon did while conducting this experiment is not healthy. The cost is too high. Living for pleasure (hedonism) leads to some very specific negative consequences.

| :: LIVING FOR PLEASURE DISTRACTS US FROM WHAT REALLY MATTERS.

After each moment of pleasure has passed, you find yourself right back where you started. As Solomon said, worshipping pleasure leaves you as empty as everything else in life apart from God. It's pointless.

Check out Solomon's shocking conclusion in Ecclesiastes 7:2:

> It is better to go to a house of mourning
>   than to go to a house of feasting,

for death is the destiny of every man;
the living should take this to heart.

In other words he's saying it's better to go to a funeral (a house of mourning) than a party where there will be laughing, singing, dancing, great food, alcohol, and all the stuff that makes us feel good.

Why in the world would such a wise man say such a terrible thing? We know from the rest of Ecclesiastes that Solomon didn't believe we should live in sadness all the time. His point is that a funeral reminds us of the most important truth about life on earth—it's very, very short. If you're living for parties and pleasure, you're wasting your short, short life on things that don't matter. Why throw away your life chasing pleasure?

2 :: LIVING FOR PLEASURE LEADS TO SLAVERY.

What started out as being enough pleasure to distract you from your meaningless life becomes less and less effective over time. You begin to need more to reach the same level of pleasure. More laughter. More pornography. More alcohol. More drugs. More TV and movies and video games. More sleep. More of whatever it is you're squeezing for relief. You can never get enough to keep yourself satisfied.

You get to the point where you have to sacrifice everything in order to look for pleasure all the time. One of the first things to go is your money. Proverbs 21:17 says, "He who loves pleasure will become poor; whoever loves wine and oil will never be rich." (Unless they stop living for those things, as Solomon did.)

What do you call someone who has to give all his time and money to something in order to keep living? A slave. Paul wrote to Titus, "At one time we too were foolish...enslaved by all kinds of passions and pleasures" (Titus 3:3).

Living for pleasure makes you a slave of pleasure.

3 :: LIVING FOR PLEASURE CAUSES CONFLICT WITH OTHER PEOPLE.

People who live only for what feels good don't care much about anyone but themselves. Some hedonists are honest about that. They'll tell you right up front that they'll ditch anyone who gets between them and feeling good.

Other pleasure lovers lie to themselves or others to try to make themselves look like good people. But they can't keep up the charade for long. James asked, "What causes fights and quarrels among you? Don't they come from your desires that battle within you?" (James 4:1). Often you have to hurt someone to get what you want to make you feel good.

Paul said to Titus that when they were slaves to pleasure and passion, one result was that they "lived in malice and envy, being hated and hating one another" (Titus 3:3).

Party animals pretend to be all about everyone having a good time and nobody getting hurt. But if you live for pleasure long enough, you'll be willing to hurt anyone to keep feeling good.

4 :: LIVING FOR PLEASURE HURTS YOUR RELATIONSHIP WITH GOD.

As we said before, not all pleasure is sin. However, if you keep pursuing pleasure, eventually you'll have to choose between doing what feels good and obeying God. Remember what led Eve to commit the very first sin? "When the woman saw that the fruit of the tree was good for food and pleasing to the eye...she took some and ate it" (Genesis 3:6).

You can't live both for pleasure and for God (2 Timothy 3:4). According to James, it ruins your motivation for praying and causes your prayers to go unanswered (James 4:3). Eventually it causes you to start living as God's enemy (James 4:4). In fact most people who live for pleasure are, simply, spiritually dead (1 Timothy 5:6).

LIVING WITH PLEASURE?

So what's the answer? After all life is full of pleasure. And pleasure does sometimes bring temporary relief from our problems. How should we as Christians live *with* pleasure in the world?

As we'll hear from Solomon over and over throughout this book, there is zero meaning in life on this earth. So we'd better find meaning in life beyond this earth. Because the only life worth living is one that's lived for God.

But people living for God can still enjoy the pleasure he gives on earth. One of Solomon's conclusions is that "a man can do nothing better than to eat and drink and find satisfaction in his work" (Ecclesiastes 2:24). That's not where meaning in life comes from, but those things can bring happiness to life when we don't expect any more than that from them.

Pleasure is best when we enjoy it and let it go. Pleasure destroys when we make it the point of our lives. One of the best ways I know to enjoy pleasure and let it go is to follow the direction of Colossians 3:17: "And whatever you do, whether in word or deed, do it all in the name of the Lord Jesus, giving thanks to God the Father through him."

So when pleasurable moments come your way—a great meal, a good laugh with friends, a perfect song, a lovemaking session when you're married, or anything else that is good and pleasurable and from God—go for it. Enjoy it like it's a sweet thing from him. Thank him for it. And then move on.

Don't expect those moments to become the point of your life. They'll disappoint you if you expect them to satisfy beyond the moment. But make God the point of your life, and each of those moments will become evidence of his great love for you— and your great future with him in heaven.

As believers it's tempting to just point to the Bible and say, "Some pleasures are good; others are bad. God said so." We believe that's true, but it's not very convincing to someone who doesn't believe in the Bible. Here are a few ideas for starting a conversation with an unbeliever about the emptiness of pleasure-seeking.

1 :: ENCOURAGE HONESTY BY BEING HONEST.

You can be open about the fact that we all love pleasure. Even if you've never had sex, you're probably interested in it. Or at least curious about it. The same goes for drinking. And drugs. And partying. You can admit there's something real and intense in pleasure.

But such honesty should go both ways. Everyone has seen examples of pleasure-seeking gone bad. Alcoholics who lose everything important in life and hurt everyone they care about. Sexual adventurers who end up with STDs and mangled relationships. Rock stars and movie icons who go to rehab and swear off everything they used to do for fun.

We don't need the Bible to see that pleasure can take a person only so far before it drags him or her down.

2 :: KEEP YOUR SENSE OF HUMOR.

Laughter can help to break down barriers between people who don't naturally agree. Learn to laugh at yourself and with those who think you're wrong about life. You can offer a reasonable defense of what you believe without being defensive.

But remember: Laughing together doesn't change the reality that life under the sun and apart from God is ultimately meaningless. Look for opportunities to point out to unbelieving friends that the pleasure of laughter has its limits. Ask if they've noticed that trying to laugh too much makes them feel empty.

3 :: BE READY TO EXPLAIN WHY YOU AVOID SOME KINDS OF PARTYING.

Remember what Peter wrote in 1 Peter 4:4? Party people don't understand why we don't indulge in every pleasure we can find. And sometimes they get mean about it. So instead of making excuses, be ready to give your friends a real answer for your party pooping ways. Talk about why you don't drink, do drugs, or sleep around.

With a close friend you trust to listen to you, you could explain you're convinced the pleasure isn't worth the cost in the long run, because it can lead to greater emptiness, addictions, conflicts with friends, and distance from God.

4 :: ASK YOUR FRIENDS WHAT THEY THINK ULTIMATELY MATTERS IN LIFE.

Find out what your unbelieving friends are living for. What do they think will bring meaning in life? Be prepared to talk about why you think living for God makes more sense than any other lifestyle. This conversation can help you explain your belief that Jesus is the only door to a life that not only matters now—but will matter forever.

OBSERVATION EXERCISES

1. For the next week, keep track of how many media stories you notice about celebrities (or real people) who are indulging in pleasure or paying for doing so. For example, you might look for stories about people going to rehab, drunk-driving citations, drug busts, or other examples of the high cost of living for pleasure.

2. Pay attention to all the things in your life that could be called pleasurable—sleeping late, eating something amazing, winning a game, finishing a project. Make a point to thank God for as many of these things as possible.

3. Watch your friends. How much pleasure or happiness do they get from music? How much pleasure do they get from laughing? Do they ever seem to be trying to get more meaning or satisfaction from those things than they can provide?

4. Observe your own heart. What pleasures (healthy or not) do you tend to lean on too much for escape, relief, or some kind of satisfaction? Do those things really satisfy you in a lasting way? How does your experience compare with Solomon's experiment with pleasure?

ROMANCE

ROMANCE AND SEX

AND SEX

Once upon a time—long before Christopher Columbus sailed the ocean blue—people believed the world was flat. Like a tabletop. They believed the horizon marked the edge of the earth. They believed the ocean flowed over the edge into nothingness. Historians tell us the flat-earth theory was developed by wrong-headed church leaders—even though the Bible doesn't teach it. Once the theory got started, people began accepting it as truth.

Even sailors bought into the myth. Imagine how they must have felt about sailing into the distance, beyond where others had gone. Imagine the nightmares they must have had about journeying past the point of no return and sailing over the edge of the world in a spectacular and deadly waterfall.

Their view of the world—literally, their "world view"—kept them from expanding their horizons... from finding new lands...from sailing with confidence through new waters of discovery. Though their hearts probably longed for exploration, they chose, instead, to follow the same paths as everyone else, afraid to do anything but stay close to home.

In other words they allowed their belief in an outdated myth to keep them from enjoying what the world had to offer.

Some people accuse Christians of making the same mistake.

They contend that living according to God's instructions is similar to believing the earth is flat. That insistence on obeying God causes Christians to play things safe...to miss out on golden opportunities...and to sacrifice our hearts' desires. They argue that our beliefs keep us from experiencing things that can open our eyes and minds to brave new worlds.

That was definitely the perspective of a 1998 movie called *Pleasantville*. In the film, Tobey Maguire and Reese Witherspoon play '90s teenagers who are magically transported into a 1950s black-and-white TV show such as *Leave It to Beaver*. Everything in the sitcom world is perfect—because no one in the squeaky clean town does anything dangerous or risky or dishonest. That is not until Reese's and Tobey's characters start breaking rules and "following their hearts." As a result color starts popping up throughout the dull, gray world they live in. They find that acting on their passions, breaking out of the norm, brings their world to vivid life.

For some characters one of the things that brings color to the world of Pleasantville is sex. Reese's character has sex with a high school basketball star. Her June Cleaver-style mom is transformed by her infatuation with a man she's not married to and by sexual experiences of her own. Suddenly, everything in her world is bursting with color. Though it's dangerous, the mom finds herself alive in a way she's never been before.

WORLD VIEW CHOICES

That's just one example. If you've been paying attention to TV, movies, and music, you've probably noticed that the popular views of sex and romantic love in the media are a lot different from those in the Bible. Here's how our culture's worldview of sex breaks down:

> Sex is a healthy, natural experience shared by any two people who want to explore it. Sex is mostly about fun, so no lifelong commitment is required. As the characters on *Friends, The OC,* and many other TV shows have discovered, sex is a normal activity for couples on their third date or fifth date or two month anniversary. Whenever a person is "ready," he or she should begin exploring the world of sex by dressing in a sexy way or watching sexy things online and elsewhere. And when the time is right, he or she should go for it.

Sex isn't the only thing that gets distorted by our culture. The idea of romantic love presented in soap operas, movies, and sitcoms also differs from the perspective you'll find in God's Word. Here's a quick breakdown of our culture's ideas concerning romantic love:

> Falling in love is something that happens to you when you least expect it. You can't help who you fall in love with. It's not something you control. When it happens you should go for it, hoping the other person shares your feelings. True love occurs when you fall in love with someone who falls in love with you, and you make a lasting, meaningful connection. You hope it lasts forever, but sadly, one or both of you will likely "fall out of love." That, of course, leads to break-ups, divorce, and sadness. The only thing to do then is to pick yourself up and start looking for true love again.

That's one way of looking at the world. One that seems about 180 degrees from reality. I believe the images of sex and romantic love promoted by our culture create a powerful deception that leads many people into a meaningless existence of wandering around in the same "safe" waters as everyone else. Never sailing off toward the horizon of the best this life has to offer. Never experiencing the ecstasy of life and love "beyond the sun."

I believe the people who buy into those perspectives regarding sex and love are the ones suffering from flat-earth syndrome. Think about it. *Their* world views are the ones based on fear. Specifically, they're afraid of missing out on things that will bring meaning, satisfaction, and lasting excitement. Their thinking goes something like this:

What if there is no life after this one? If God isn't real or trustworthy, then my only hope is to get all I can out of sex and earthly love before I die. I'm afraid not to try it all, because I might miss out. Don't ask me to sail too far toward a God who may not be there.

Our worldview—what we really believe in our hearts to be true about life—determines how we live and the choices we make. So someone who's convinced that the God of the Bible does not exist or may not be trustworthy will be open to finding something that works without him. So why not indulge in sexual experiences in high school? Why not hope for an earthly relationship to fill an empty soul? Why not try anything and everything?

On the other hand, a person who's convinced God is real and the Bible is his Word to us will be open to living a riskier life of trusting him. If the Designer says sex is a wonderful gift intended to bind two people in heterosexual marriage, I step away from the comfort zone of my own understanding...and wait. If the Creator says romantic love is not something that just happens to people, but a choice you make to commit yourself to another person for life, I sail away from infatuations with the wrong people and set my course for a relationship based on his kind of love.

SOLOMON: KING OF SEX AND ROMANCE

For all of his supernatural wisdom, Solomon lacked the courage to believe that God's way was best. The book of Ecclesiastes offers us the opportunity to learn from Solomon's mistake. Like many of us, Solomon said, "I'm not sure which world view to believe yet. I want to try them all to see what works for me."

And believe me, Solomon tried it *all*. The man didn't hold back when it came to experiencing both sex and romance. Check out what 1 Kings 11:1-2 tells us about Solomon's love life:

> King Solomon, however, loved many foreign women besides Pharaoh's daughter—Moabites, Ammonites, Edomites, Sidonians and Hittites. They were from nations about which the LORD had told the Israelites, "You must not intermarry with them, because they will surely turn your hearts after their gods." Nevertheless, Solomon held fast to them in love.

In spite of the fact that God told Solomon's people not to marry foreigners because they worshipped idols, Solomon hooked up with one foreign woman after another. We know that he didn't start out with the intention of turning his back on God. Solomon knew God had honored his dad David for following him. And as a young king, Solomon believed the God of Israel was the only true God, the only source of real power.

But Solomon was afraid to believe God completely in the area of sex and romance. He seems to have been afraid to leave the "safe water" of his culture's worldview for two reasons. First, marrying the daughters of foreign kings was the strategy his culture recommended for making peace and building financial success. Solomon figured the king of Egypt (Pharaoh) would be less likely to attack Israel if his daughter lived in the king's palace. And he figured if that strategy worked with Egypt, why not marry as many princesses as he possibly could?

You can see the logic in his culture's worldview. Most kings would do the same thing if they could. Solomon knew God said it was wrong, but he was afraid to trust God alone to protect him and his kingdom. So he married foreign wives. A *lot* of them.

The second likely reason Solomon married so many wives and collected so many concubines (women who were used for sex) is that he was afraid of missing out on any sexual or romantic experience. Remember, Solomon was searching for anything under the sun that might bring meaning to life. So he pursued all the sex and all the romance he could find.

Let's just say Hugh Hefner's Playboy Mansion had nothing on Solomon's palace. In Ecclesiastes 2:8 Solomon tells us, "I acquired...a harem as well—the delights of the heart of man." A Middle Eastern harem was a group of women who were kept by a rich man or a king for the purpose of sex. First Kings 11:3 tells us Solomon had access to "seven hundred wives of royal birth and three hundred concubines."

That's a lot of women. And a lot of sex. The fact that these descriptions come from the Bible doesn't mean they're somehow more noble or less sexual than they appear to be. Remember, Solomon was trying *everything*. He had a rep as a man with a huge sexual appetite. And he had the power to make his every fantasy come true. So we can assume he engaged in all kinds of sex with all 1,000 of his women—and not just one at a time.

And what did Solomon conclude about his playboy lifestyle? "I denied myself nothing my eyes desired; I refused my heart no pleasure. Yet...everything was meaningless, a chasing after the wind; nothing was gained under the sun" (Ecclesiastes 2:10-11).

Don't misunderstand—Solomon had a good time. He called his sexual adventures the "delights of the heart of man" (Ecclesiastes 2:8). He enjoyed the sex. But after a lifetime of sexual experiences with all kinds of exotic women, he discovered his life was just as empty as ever. The best sex the world had to offer wasn't enough to satisfy him.

His message to us is simple: Don't bother looking for a meaningful life in sexual pleasure. You won't find anything there but emptiness.

Some of you may be saying, "I don't want a harem. And I certainly don't want to *be* in a harem. I'm not interested in having sex with a thousand people. I just want a boyfriend or girlfriend. I want romance and true love. I want to feel connected to another person in a meaningful way."

Believe it or not, that's what Solomon wanted too. Even with all of his wives and concubines, he was a romantic at heart. The poet-king had a beautiful, sensitive, artistic soul. He loved his wives. Imagine some of the weddings he must have thrown for them. Most of the brides were princesses after all. The finest clothes. Huge parties. Hundreds of attendants. Thousands of guests. Parades. Feasts. Lavish wedding nights.

If you doubt the poet-king was truly a romantic guy, check out Song of Songs (also known as Song of Solomon) in your Bible. In this book Solomon uses beautiful, romantic imagery to describe his relationship with a young, country girl who worked in a vineyard. She was probably just a teenager, and he fell hard for her. Remember, this was a different culture. One in which people expected the king to have many wives. Young women considered it an honor to be one of them. In the book the young girl and Solomon meet, grow close, and long to be together.

Solomon and his love become united—both romantically and sexually. Together they experience everything that earthly love has to offer. What could be more romantic for a young lady than to be noticed and courted by a wealthy, handsome, and powerful king?

Apparently the young woman couldn't stop talking to her friends about her royal beau: "My lover is radiant and ruddy, outstanding among ten thousand. His head is purest gold; his hair is wavy and black as a raven. His eyes are like doves by the water streams, washed in milk, mounted like jewels" (Song of Songs 5:10-12).

She goes on and on like that about him. And the king talks endlessly and poetically about her as well. Eventually, she says to her friends, "This is my lover, this is my friend" (Song of Songs 5:16). What could be more perfect?

Still when Solomon gets older, he can't identify anything in life that has meaning. And that includes earthly romance, relationships, and marriage. Later in Ecclesiastes, Solomon says loving your wife, enjoying your relationships, and walking with companions is a good thing—a gift from God. But it's not enough to fill the emptiness of life without him.

In his great experiment, Solomon reports that neither passionate romance nor unlimited sex can provide the satisfaction or meaning in life he was looking for. In fact choosing to follow his culture instead of fearlessly following God's plan for sex and marriage cost Solomon greatly in his life.

If we're smart we'll learn from his mistake. You see, there's still a price to pay for not trusting the Creator of sex and romance.

THE HIGH COST OF REJECTING GOD'S DESIGN

God's plan for sex, love, and marriage doesn't guarantee you a meaningful and happy life. (Go ahead and read that last sentence again, just to make sure you saw it right.) I believe some Christian teachers mislead young believers into thinking Christian marriage provides ultimate satisfaction in life.

That's not true. According to God's Word in Ecclesiastes, *nothing* on earth provides ultimate meaning or satisfaction. That includes a God-honoring marriage relationship. But—and this is a big *but*—living according to the Creator's design when it comes to love, sex, and marriage does provide some very good things in life.

Let's get specific. What exactly is God's plan for Christians today? For starters he says sex is intended for heterosexual marriage and nothing else. The writer of Hebrews says, "Marriage should be honored by all, and the marriage bed kept pure" (Hebrews 13:4). In that relationship sex becomes not just pleasure (though there's plenty of that), but part of God's plan for binding two people together emotionally, physically, and even spiritually. In other words sex can create both excitement and closeness between two people for life.

And what about romantic love? The God of the Bible is all for it. His Word is full of stories about men and women who found each other and committed themselves to one another for life. What could be more romantic than that? But nothing in the Bible suggests that somewhere out there is *the one* you're meant to be with. There's no reason to believe the Hollywood notion that if you don't find *the one*, you'll miss out on true happiness for life.

Instead, all of God's instructions about marriage involve loving and respecting the person you married. Even when life gets hard. Even when feelings of love come and go. In other words the Designer of romantic love asks us to control it instead of being controlled by it. His Word does *not* teach that love is something that happens to you. You can and should control who you give yourself to in love and who you don't.

God warns Christians not to connect ourselves in marriage with people who are not Christians (2 Corinthians 6:14). He also makes it clear that marriage is a lifelong commitment, which means divorce is not an option for those looking for God's best from marriage.

Here's the bottom line. God wants his people to enjoy romance and marriage. But more important, he wants us to live for him. In a culture that seems to say the path to true happiness involves finding your one perfect mate and having lots of great sex, many people are afraid to trust God's plan. They don't want to miss out. And they end up paying a heavy price for choosing the risky path of not believing the Designer. Here's how:

1 :: REJECTING GOD'S PLAN FOR SEX AND ROMANCE DAMAGES YOUR RELATIONSHIP WITH HIM.

"Okay, I'm a good Christian, and I love God and everything. But there's this person I'm dating..."

How many times have you heard that? How many times have you said (or thought) it?

Finding someone you can't imagine letting go of can play havoc with your emotions. Especially if the person isn't a Christian. Or if the person doesn't live for God. Or if the person is already married.

That's when the excuses come out:

- "But we're in love!"

- "We're perfect together!"

- "This doesn't feel wrong."

- "If I give him or her up, I may never find true happiness again."

No one ever said trusting God's plan would be easy. But it will save you from a world of trouble. Just ask Solomon—who made the wrong choice over and over and over and ended up paying a high price for his lack of faith.

People tell me all the time that dating a non-Christian won't change their relationship with God. But it *always* does. Most of the foreign women Solomon married didn't believe in the one true God. Yet Solomon married them anyway. And 1 Kings 11:4-6 describes what happened:

> As Solomon grew old, his wives turned his heart after other gods, and his heart was not fully devoted to the LORD his God, as the heart of David his father had been. He followed Ashtoreth the goddess of the Sidonians, and Molech the detestable god of the Ammonites. So Solomon did evil in the eyes of the Lord; he did not follow the Lord completely, as David his father had done.

When you love someone, you will be drawn to the things they love. It's just something that happens. Solomon was drawn toward the gods his wives loved, just as God said he would be.

Solomon didn't reject God completely. He just stopped being fully devoted to him. He moved his relationship with God out of the first spot in his life. And when you do that, something else will take God's place.

In Solomon's case that something else turned out to be some of the worst demons and false gods in ancient history. The king imported them into Israel. Instead of protecting God's people

from evil, he introduced them to it. Solomon followed his une-
qually yoked wives away from God.

That doesn't mean if you date a non-Christian, you'll end up
worshiping demons. God's point is that if you move your relationship with him out of the top place in your heart, there's no
telling how far you'll walk away from his best path for you.

2 :: REJECTING GOD'S PLAN FOR SEX AND ROMANCE COSTS YOU PEACE OF MIND.

Although Ecclesiastes makes it clear that we will not find ultimate meaning or satisfaction in this life under the sun, we can
find some extremely valuable things in the God who gives gifts
from "beyond the sun." One of those things is peace.

For Solomon, that peace was political and military. God gave
Solomon—and Israel—decades without war, without conflict,
without battles. But when Solomon rejected God's plan, God
took away Israel's political peace. If you read the rest of 1 Kings
11, you'll see that God raised up several enemies for Solomon to
worry about in his old age.

Even in our meaningless lives under the sun, the Bible tells
us that Christians can have peace. For one thing we have peace
with God because Jesus died to pay for our sins. Therefore, we're
forgiven (Romans 5:1-2). We can also have peace of mind. In his
letter to the Christians living in Philippi, Paul describes how we
can have a peace unbelievers will never understand. All we have
to do is take our prayer requests to God and give him thanks for
meeting our needs (Philippians 4:4-7).

But when you reject God's plan and disobey him in the way
you approach romance and sex, it's hard to have that conversation. It's hard to take your requests to him and thank him for
providing good gifts to you, because you've rejected those gifts in

a key area of your life. Getting what you want, romantically and sexually, can't give you the peace of mind you can have by walking closely with the Father.

3 :: REJECTING GOD'S PLAN COSTS STABLE RELATIONSHIPS AND DEEPER INTIMACY.

If you buy in to our culture's view that love can come without warning and leave just as quickly, then no relationship is safe. Break-ups and divorce are always options. And those options lead to lasting scars, broken homes, damaged kids, and unbelievable pain.

Too often I've heard people say, "I'm just not happy anymore," when they talk about their relationships. Their idea is that good relationships always make people happy. Therefore, if yours isn't making you happy, you need to get out of it. Solomon says the sad truth about life on earth is that happiness isn't permanent. So no relationship is ever going to leave anyone feeling perfectly happy all the time.

God's plan for marriage is for two people to sail together toward the horizon. He wants spouses to understand their job in the relationship is to give to the other person, not to get something to satisfy themselves. He wants them to understand their marriage is meant to be a little glimpse of the relationship between Jesus and Christians everywhere—a relationship that's not going to end.

4 :: REJECTING GOD'S PLAN COSTS YOU AN ULTIMATELY SATISFYING SEX LIFE.

Some people may be thinking, *Well, all that might be true, but I don't care. I've got to have sex. I've got to try all kinds of sex. I've got to be a player. I might not be tight with God or have peace of mind or stable relationships, but at least, I'll have great sex.*

Turns out, that's not true. According to the *Atlantic Monthly* September 2004 coverage of a study conducted by the National Bureau of Economic Research, "Married people have considerably more sex than swinging singles and gay divorcees, and the 'happiness-maximizing' number of sexual partners in a given year is almost exactly one."

Many surveys have shown the same thing. The ones having the most sex—and liking it best—are married people who have sex only with their spouses! How wild is that? Married people are having more and better sex than people who are trying to find satisfaction in life by having all the sex they can.

Solomon tells us there's no ultimate meaning or satisfaction in sex or romance. But people who live according to God's plan can find real enjoyment and closeness in experiencing those things together.

HOW TO TALK TO UNBELIEVING FRIENDS ABOUT THE SEARCH FOR MEANING IN SEX AND ROMANCE

The desire for sex and romance is one reason many people reject God when they're young. They don't want to be told what to do, sexually speaking, or who to fall in love with. However, Solomon doesn't tell anyone to keep sex inside of marriage or to avoid romance that leads you away from God. In fact he broke the rules himself. He simply tells us those things don't lead to anything that matters.

1 :: ASK YOUR FRIENDS HOW THEY FEEL ABOUT THE BIBLE'S RESTRICTIONS ON SEX AND MARRIAGE.

Obviously these questions are not intended for casual conversation, but for more serious exchanges with people you know pretty well. Do your friends feel the biblical or "religious" rules about sex outside of marriage, homosexuality, and romantic love are pointless? Or do they recognize that there are reasons behind the Bible's guidelines? Be prepared to describe why you think God put those guidelines in place.

2 :: ASK YOUR FRIENDS IF THEY SEE A DOWNSIDE TO TOO MUCH SEX OR UNHEALTHY ROMANCE.

Rather than asking your friends to share potentially embarrassing personal stories, have them consider the question from the perspective of observing the world around them. Have they seen people burned by overindulgence in sex and romance? How about in the larger world of celebrities and the media? Do they believe people famous for having multiple sex and marriage partners ever pay a price for their lifestyles? Do they believe those people are respected for their experiences?

3 :: ASK YOUR FRIENDS HOW THEY FEEL ABOUT SEX AND ROMANCE AS PART OF MARRIAGE.

Do they believe romance and sex within the Bible's limits can still be rewarding and fulfilling? Why or why not? Do they believe there are any advantages to exclusive sexual and romantic relationships? Be sure to offer your opinion. If you think it would be helpful, mention the survey cited at the end of the chapter.

OBSERVATION EXERCISES

1. As you look at your friends and the people in your life, how much priority do you think they give sex and romance? Would most of them mention one or both as the most important things in their lives? Would they put them in the top three? How about the top ten? Why do you think sex and romance play such big parts in the search for meaning and satisfaction among students? Have any of your friends or schoolmates been burned by placing too much priority on sex or romance?

2. Do a little counting this week. What percentage of the songs you hear have something to do with sex or romance—including songs about break-ups? What percentage of the TV shows and movies you watch have to do with sex or romance? What percentage of the conversations you have with people your own age include discussions about sex or romance? How many of those songs, shows, movies, or conversations seem to place some hope on finding happiness through sex or romance?

3. How would your life be different if sex and romantic love were not such a huge part of our culture? Think about it. How would things be different if sex weren't used in so many ads, shows, movies, and songs? If it weren't so easy to access on the Internet? If romantic books and magazines weren't in the checkout lanes of every grocery store? How would it change what happens in your mind and in the world around you? Why do you think so?

4. Observe your own heart. It's totally normal for students to be interested in sex and romantic love. That's not wrong. But ask yourself this: How much hope are you placing on finding meaning or satisfaction in life through sex or romance someday? Do you think your life will be more complete once you experience one or both? Why or why not? Can a person live a fully satisfying life without ever experiencing true romance or sex? Explain.

I WANT

I WANT MORE

MORE

On Christmas Day 2002, Jack and Jewell Whittaker lived out the fantasy of millions of people all over the world. That's the day the West Virginia couple won the biggest single lottery payout ever: $314 million. After taxes, their lump-sum payout was a giant check for $113 million. Talk about the best Christmas ever!

On TV Jack and Jewell looked happy. Why wouldn't they be, right? In his big cowboy hat and boots, Jack laughed and promised to do all the things people tell themselves they'd do if God would let them win the lottery. And Jack made good on his promise.

In the months that followed, the Whittakers gave $7 million to three local churches. They started a charity to help people find jobs, go to college, and get food. They built a neighborhood playground. They bought coloring books for needy children. And after all that, they still had millions of dollars to enjoy with their family. Most people would agree they were set for life.

So why, just two short years later, did Jewell Whittaker tell the *Charleston Gazette:* "I wish all of this never would have happened. I wish I would have torn the ticket up"?

Turns out all that money wasn't such a good thing for the Whittaker family. Jack Whittaker, who apparently had lived a pretty clean life before winning the lottery, has since been arrested twice for drunk driving and ordered to go to rehab. He's developed a major gambling problem. He's gotten into countless fights. He's become a regular at local strip clubs. He's been robbed repeatedly. And one of his grandkids has disappeared. His personal and family life is in almost constant turmoil.

From the outside looking in, it seems as though Jack and his family have discovered what Solomon found to be true in his own life: Money isn't enough. Not even if you're mind-blowingly wealthy. All money does is allow you to "chase the wind" in a nicer car—and cause you to look for other ways to find relief and satisfaction.

Some of you may be thinking, *Maybe the problem wasn't the money. Maybe it was Jack. Maybe he just didn't know how to enjoy his wealth. Maybe he just wasn't smart with it. After all the millionaires I see in Hollywood and in the rap world look pretty happy with their money. I'll bet things would be different for me if I won the lottery.*

Let's hear from a few other "winners":

- "I wish it never happened. It was totally a nightmare," said William Post, who won $16.2 million in the Pennsylvania lottery and now lives on only $450 a month and food stamps.

- "Winning the lottery isn't always what it's cracked up to be," said Evelyn Adams, who won the New Jersey lottery twice and now lives in a trailer.

- Suzanne Williams won $4.2 million in the Virginia lottery in 1993 and is now deeper in debt than she was before she won.

To help people like these, Susan Bradley started a company called the Sudden Money* Institute. She says part of the problem is that people who win the lottery or suddenly inherit millions of dollars believe the same lie many of us do.

"In our culture there is a widely held belief that money solves problems," she says. "People think if they had more money, their troubles would be over. When a family receives sudden money, they frequently learn that money can cause as many problems as it solves."

Of course not everyone who becomes a millionaire loses it all or starts drinking heavily. But every millionaire knows what Solomon knew: Money can't pay for a satisfying life, lasting meaning, or inner peace.

THE RICHES OF SOLOMON

If you've seen the movie *National Treasure*, you know that a big chunk of the hidden fortune the treasure hunters are looking for is supposed to have come from Solomon's palace. Of course that's a fictional idea—but it has the ring of truth because Solomon may have been the most loaded guy who ever lived. You could say he was big into bling.

First Kings 10 reads like an ancient script for MTV's *Cribs*, with its awe-inspiring peek into Solomon's lifestyle. Here's what we know about the Bling King. Translating numbers into

American dollars, he took in over $300 million every year...in gold alone. He had gold everything—cups, household items, military shields, not to mention his throne. His enormous, one-of-a-kind seat of power had six steps leading up to it, with a pair of lions on each step and another pair beside the armrests. Nothing like it had ever been made before—and nothing like it has been made since.

The magnificent temple he built for God was recognized as one of the seven wonders of the ancient world. And the palace he built for himself was even bigger and more spectacular. Solomon's crib must have seemed like a museum, with all of its fine woods, gold, and rare, priceless gifts from admirers around the world.

You want to know how rich Solomon was? He had so much silver lying around his kingdom that the precious metal became as worthless as rocks on the street.

Like today's celebrity millionaires, Solomon loved his transportation. But having a dozen or so quality rides in his garage wasn't enough for him. Solomon had to build entire *cities* just to hold his 1,400 chariots and drivers and 12,000 horses.

The king also had some nice vacation digs when he needed to get away from the pressures of the palace. Check out what Bible scholar and historian G. Frederick Owen wrote about one of those retreats—and how Solomon displayed his wealth:

> Solomon literally built himself a paradise of pleasure. One of his chief resorts was Etham where, when the mornings were beautiful, he often went in stately progress, "dressed in snow white raiment, riding in his chariot of state, which was made of the finest cedar, decked with gold and silver and purple, and carpeted with the costliest tapestry worked by the daughters of Jerusalem; and attended by a bodyguard of sixty val-

iant men of the tallest and handsomest of the young men of Israel, arrayed in Tyrian purple, with their long, black hair, freshly sprinkled with gold dust every day, glittering in the sun." (*Abraham to Middle-East Crisis,* Eerdmans, 1957)

Paints quite a picture, doesn't it? Those rap videos with the Rolls Royces, gold jewelry, and beautiful people everywhere have nothing on Solomon's style. He rolled in total luxury and excess everywhere he went.

On top of all of that, Solomon's household cost millions just to run. It was full of the best and brightest in the land, all working together like clockwork to make the king happy. And all of those people—the officials, the servants, the wives, the kids, the visitors from around the world—had to be fed and clothed and housed. Here's what 1 Kings 4:22-23 tells us about life at the palace:

> Solomon's daily provisions were thirty cors [over 1,700 gallons] of fine flour and sixty cors [almost 3,500 gallons] of meal, ten head of stall-fed cattle, twenty of pasture-fed cattle and a hundred sheep and goats, as well as deer, gazelles, roebucks and choice fowl.

We're talking about tons of the best food in the region, prepared by the best cooks, being consumed every day.

The queen of Sheba is well known in history for her incredible wealth and luxurious lifestyle. Yet the things she heard about Solomon—specifically about his wisdom and riches—intrigued even her. Eventually she decided to visit Jerusalem to see Solomon's kingdom for herself. She arrived with a huge, camel-powered caravan to check out Solomon's riches and test his wisdom with hard questions. We're told she was blown away by what she discovered.

When the queen of Sheba saw all the wisdom of Solomon and the palace he had built, the food on his table, the seating of his officials, the attending servants in their robes, his cupbearers, and the burnt offerings he made at the temple of the LORD, she was overwhelmed.

She said to the king..."I did not believe these things until I came and saw with my own eyes. Indeed, not even half was told me; in wisdom and wealth you have far exceeded the report I heard" (1 Kings 10:4-7).

MONEY FAILS

Okay, so we know Solomon wasn't hurting for pocket change. Not only did he inherit a fortune from his father, he worked his tail off to create an even more massive fortune. In other words he received money as a gift, and he earned it. That's what makes his conclusions about looking for meaning in money interesting—and reliable.

If Solomon had been just a poor monk, on a mountaintop somewhere, spouting off about money not satisfying the longings of the heart, we might not listen as closely. But when a guy who could buy and sell the world tells us "this too is meaningless," we should probably pay attention.

In the book of Ecclesiastes, Solomon identifies at least seven reasons why money fails to fulfill our search for real and lasting satisfaction.

1 :: EVENTUALLY SOMEONE ELSE WILL CONTROL EVERYTHING YOU'VE WORKED FOR.

While most people agree it's a good thing for parents or grandparents to be able to leave something behind for their kids, Solomon pointed out that it's also unfair.

Look at his words in Ecclesiastes 2:21: "For a man may do his work with wisdom, knowledge, and skill, and then he must leave all he owns to someone who has not worked for it. This too is meaningless and a great misfortune." Who knows what the inheritor will do with his unearned wealth? Or as Solomon asked in Ecclesiastes 2:19, "Who knows whether he will be a wise man or a fool?"

Consider the life and legacy of Conrad Hilton, the man who worked his entire life to build the Hilton Hotel international business empire. Conrad Hilton died in 1979 and left his fortune to his children, grandchildren, and great-grandchildren, including Paris and Nicky Hilton.

How do you think Ol' Conrad would have felt about leaving Paris and Nicky each about $28 million if he could have looked into the future and seen their lifestyles? Do you think he would have worked quite as hard to make his fortune if he had known what his heirs would do with it?

2 :: MUCH OF YOUR MONEY GOES STRAIGHT TO THE GOVERNMENT.

Even though Solomon was part of the problem in his kingdom, he saw how poor people were being oppressed by the government. According to Ecclesiastes 5:8-9, government corruption involving taxes was a big problem in Israel. Every government official, from the lowest administrator all the way up to the king, took a piece of the working person's wages.

The same thing happens today in almost every country in the world. We pay sales tax, city tax, property tax, state income tax, and federal income tax. And politicians find ways to divide the proceeds among themselves. One organization calculates that every year, most Americans have to work until sometime in April just to make enough money to pay their annual taxes. In other words every dime you make until April goes to the government in one form or another. After that, you finally start earning for yourself.

There's no way around the problem for us working stiffs. Jesus made it very clear that we should pay our taxes (Mark 12:13-17). So we're left with Solomon's conclusion; money fails to satisfy, because we spend so much time working to give it to other people.

3 :: THERE'S NO SUCH THING AS ENOUGH.

Solomon left little room for debate on this point. Look at his words in Ecclesiastes 5:10: "Whoever loves money never has money enough; whoever loves wealth is never satisfied with his income."

One of the biggest problems with living for riches is that there's no finish line. You never get to a comfortable place. Someone who lives to find satisfaction through wealth never wakes up one morning and says, "Now I'm good."

I know a handful of multi-millionaires, and they all have lots of cool stuff. Many of them fly to work in helicopters and live in mansions. But do you know what they talk about when you sit around the table with them? Everything is so expensive. The price of gasoline is on the rise. Taxes are high.

They're still worried about money. They haven't yet reached the place where they can say, "I'm rich. I don't care what anything costs." You might one day have millions of dollars too. But if you're living for money, you'll still think you need more.

4 :: HAVING MONEY IS EXPENSIVE.

Solomon put it this way in Ecclesiastes 5:11: "As goods increase, so do those who consume them. And what benefit are they to the owner except to feast his eyes on them."

Maybe King Bling looked around his room as he wrote those words and noticed all of the expensive gold objects he had everywhere. Maybe he started thinking about how much he was paying people to design the objects...create them...clean them...repair them...and replace them. Maybe he became frustrated, because after all that, all he could do was look at his objects. None of them could do anything else for him.

Susan Bradley of the Sudden Money® Institute says, "A lot of people who don't have money don't realize how much it costs to live in a big house—decorators, furniture, taxes, insurance, even utility costs are greater."

And that's true for everything you own. Having nice stuff always costs more than the initial price you pay for it. For one thing it takes its toll in stress, because you have to take care of your possessions, update them, fix them, and—eventually—sell them.

In Ecclesiastes 5:12 Solomon says, "The sleep of the laborer is sweet, whether he eats little or much, but the abundance of a rich man permits him no sleep." What's the point of being rich, the king argues, if it robs you of rest?

5 :: STORING UP A LOT OF MONEY IS WORTHLESS.

When I was in grade school, I bought the *Guinness Book of World Records* and read it from cover to cover. I'll never forget the entry about the world's greatest miser. This woman lived in the 1800s and had millions in the bank, which was an enormous amount for that time. But the woman died in a freezing apartment from the effects of malnutrition, because she wouldn't spend money to eat properly or heat her home.

Here's what Solomon had to say about that mindset: "I have seen a grievous evil under the sun: wealth hoarded to the harm of its owner" (Ecclesiastes 5:13). Solomon knew all too well what the desire to hold on to money can do.

6 :: MONEY CAN QUICKLY VANISH.

If you've ever watched an episode of VH-1's *Behind the Music*, you know how the story goes. Band members come together from dirt-poor backgrounds. Band members create a hit song. Band members get rich. Band members party, buy cool stuff, and do a lot of drugs. Band members wake up one morning to find everything they had is gone.

The "wealth lost through some misfortune" that Solomon mentions in Ecclesiastes 5:14 covers more than just excessive partying. Money can be lost as a result of medical bills...business failure...legal troubles...bad economy...and hundreds of other factors.

Solomon knew that money sometimes can be made very quickly, but more often it is lost very quickly. He knew that holding onto money is not a reliable goal.

7 :: YOU CAN'T TAKE IT WITH YOU.

Finally Solomon describes the biggest problem facing people who look to money for real meaning or satisfaction in life: Death. The harsh reality of death turns a fat bank account into a worthless asset.

Years ago a popular bumper sticker read, "He who dies with the most toys wins." Eventually another bumper sticker could be seen countering that philosophy: "He who dies with the most toys...still dies." Solomon might have slapped the second bumper sticker on his chariot—if it were available in gold.

In Ecclesiastes 5:15-17, the poet-king describes a man who discovers the truth about money too late:

> Naked a man comes from his mother's womb,
> and as he comes, so he departs.
> He takes nothing from his labor
> that he can carry in his hand.

> This too is a grievous evil:

> As a man comes, so he departs,
> and what does he gain,
> since he toils for the wind?
> All his days he eats in darkness,
> with great frustration, affliction and anger.

Those are the results of a life lived for money: frustration, affliction, and anger. They're not words that usually come to mind when you think of the extremely rich, are they?

That's certainly not the experience of every wealthy person. The Bible never teaches that having lots of money is a sin. Solomon and the apostle Paul agree that it's the *love* of money that leads to anger, frustration, and every kind of evil.

HOW TO LIVE *WITH* MONEY

Most of us who read this chapter understand that money will never satisfy us, never solve our real problems, and never give us a meaningful life. But we'd still rather have it than not have it, wouldn't we? Let's face it, after all of his talk about the meaninglessness of wealth, Solomon didn't sell his palace and move into a van down by the river, did he? He didn't reject his money. And he doesn't tell us to reject money either.

Solomon's point—and the point of this chapter—is that we need to reject money as a motivation for how we live our lives. Solomon wants us to take money off our lists of *if onlys*. "If only I had more money, I'd be okay" is a lie.

Most of us will have to work for a living. We'll have to make money, and we'll have to spend money. We'll have to decide how hard to work to get the clothes we want and the electronic gadgets we love—not to mention that great big grill from the store. We'll need to decide how we can live with (or without) money and not make it the central point of our lives.

Solomon gives us a few ideas.

1 :: THANK GOD FOR WHAT YOU HAVE.

"Then I realized that it is good and proper for a man to eat and drink, and to find satisfaction in his toilsome labor under the sun during the few days of life God has given him—for that is his lot." You'll find those words in Ecclesiastes 5:18.

The key to living happily with money is to recognize that the cool stuff we have is a gift. A gift from God himself. He has given us everything good we have. And if that truth doesn't amaze you, you need to keep thinking about it until it does.

Unfortunately for us, it's easy to look past the good things in our lives to the good things in other people's lives. "Yeah, my car is pretty dependable, but her car is brand new!" "Yeah, my iPod is small, but his is tiny! I want that!" Solomon identified envy as the reason people work so hard for money (Ecclesiastes 4:4). We want what other people have.

The best way to combat envy is to exercise the discipline of giving thanks. And that requires some serious work. In order to develop a consistently thankful spirit, you have to slow down enough to recognize the good things in your life and then give credit where credit is due.

One of the reasons we get so wrapped up in materialism is that we don't appreciate the stuff we have right in front of us. The apostle Paul said we should give thanks for everything all the time (1 Thessalonians 5:18). If you practice the discipline of giving thanks for everything you have right now, you may start to feel embarrassed about how much great stuff you have. Even better, you won't have as much time to think about all the great stuff someone else has. You see, giving thanks turns envy into gratitude.

2 :: ENJOY WHAT YOU HAVE.

After you've practiced the hard work of giving thanks for the good things in your life, practice the fun work of enjoying them. Solomon says it over and over—the best thing anyone can do in life under the sun is to enjoy what God gives.

Think about the things on your thanksgiving list. How often do you take the time and energy to really have fun with those things? To use them in ways that make them worthwhile to you? Remember, that's what they're for.

In the first few verses of Ecclesiastes 6, Solomon reveals the difference between someone who lives *for* money and possessions and someone who lives *with* those things. The difference is enjoyment. Someone who lives *with* possessions, but not *for* them, can enjoy them. Someone who worships money or things can't really enjoy them, because he or she isn't ever satisfied with them.

Check out what Paul told a young pastor named Timothy about money and enjoyment: "Command those who are rich in this present world not to be arrogant nor to put their hope in wealth, which is so uncertain, but to put their hope in God, who richly provides us with everything for our enjoyment" (1 Timothy 6:17).

God wants you to enjoy the good things you have. So get busy and have fun and thank him for it!

3 :: CHOOSE CONTENTMENT.

We're all faced with three choices when it comes to contentment: the no-handfuls approach, the one-handful approach, and the two-handfuls approach.

The no-handfuls approach can be summed up this way: Since money can never satisfy us, there's no reason to work in order to earn it. However, that philosophy doesn't cut it in Scripture. Ecclesiastes 4:5 says, "The fool folds his hands and ruins himself."

We can't just drop out of the world of employment. In the New Testament, Paul said those in the Christian communities who didn't work shouldn't be allowed to eat in those communities (2 Thessalonians 3:10). Keep in mind, there's a difference between not living for money and not living at all!

The two-handfuls approach urges us to "go for the money" with everything we've got. To put wealth and possessions at the top of our priority lists. To refuse to rest until we have all we want. Even though we'll never have all we truly want.

As you've probably guessed, the two-handfuls approach to contentment isn't really an option for Christians. In his first letter to Timothy, Paul warns that chasing money can ruin a Christian's life. "People who want to get rich fall into temptation and a trap and into many foolish and harmful desires that plunge men into ruin and destruction.... Some people, eager for money, have wandered from the faith and pierced themselves with many griefs" (1 Timothy 6:9-10).

That leaves us with the one-handful approach. Ecclesiastes 4:6 says, "Better one handful with tranquillity than two handfuls with toil and chasing after the wind."

Solomon tells us working enough for *one* handful is the way to live *with* money and things, as opposed to living *for* them. The key to tranquillity, or a restful mind, is not to make getting rich the point of your life. Instead we should work to meet our needs. Period. Striving for any more than that isn't going to bring meaning to our lives.

Paul agreed with Solomon's recommendation. In 1 Timothy 6:6-8, he writes, "But godliness with contentment is great gain. For we brought nothing into the world, and we can take nothing out of it. But if we have food and clothing, we will be content with that."

All we really *need* is food, clothing, and shelter. Most of us in the United States have way more than that. And that's great. Having more than we need is not a problem. *Living* for more is a problem—a problem that leads to destruction, anger, frustration, and sadness.

Ч :: GIVE IT AWAY.

In Ecclesiastes 4:8, Solomon paints a picture of a greedy man: "There was a man all alone; he had neither son nor brother. There was no end to his toil, yet his eyes were not content with his wealth."

Do you know anyone like that? If you've ever read Charles Dickens' *A Christmas Carol* or seen a movie version of it, you may recognize the character of Ebenezer Scrooge in Solomon's words. In the story Scrooge is a miser who cares about nothing but money. On Christmas Eve he's visited by three ghosts, who show him how his greediness and love of money has made his life miserable.

At the end of the story, Scrooge recognizes his mistakes. And so does the greedy man Solomon describes. Look at the end of Ecclesiastes 4:8: "'For whom am I toiling,' he asked, 'and why am I depriving myself of enjoyment?' This too is meaningless—a miserable business!"

In *A Christmas Carol*, Ebenezer Scrooge is given a second chance to do something good with his money. And he takes advantage of it in a big way, spending his cash on gifts and good things for people in need. Solomon recommends the same course of action. His words in Ecclesiastes 4:9-12 make it clear that the best way to enjoy your money is to share it with other people.

The apostle Paul seconded that notion in his letter to Timothy: "Command them to do good, to be rich in good deeds, and to be generous and willing to share" (1 Timothy 6:18). In other words a great way to make sure you're not living for money is to give it away.

5 :: SERVE GOD FIRST.

You'll notice that Solomon never tells us it's wrong to want things. God doesn't expect us to become robots with no desires for anything. But he does expect us to recognize when our desire for things starts to take over our lives.

The best way to avoid the dead-end of living for material possessions is to make sure we're living for something—make that some*one*—else: the God who gives us so many good things.

Jesus put it this way: "No one can serve two masters. Either he will hate the one and love the other, or he will be devoted to the one and despise the other. You cannot serve both God and Money" (Matthew 6:24).

Living for money and stuff is not only a dead end in the search for meaning, it's a bad investment of your life.

HOW TO TALK TO UNBELIEVING FRIENDS ABOUT LIVING FOR MONEY

Money is a pretty easy subject to talk about with unbelieving friends and family. You don't have to believe in the Bible as God's Word to agree that money fails to satisfy the desire for meaning in life.

1 :: ASK YOUR FRIENDS IF THEY EVER DREAM OF WINNING THE LOTTERY.

If you do too, be honest. Ask what they would do with their winnings. How much would they save, spend, give away? What would they buy first? Be ready to share your answers to those same questions.

Then talk about some of the lottery winners mentioned at the start of this chapter. Ask your friends' opinions about why some people who come into sudden money end up worse off than they were before they struck it rich? Ask them if they believe money can solve real problems. Be ready to share the perspective that money doesn't offer real meaning in life.

2 :: TALK TO YOUR FRIENDS ABOUT SOME OF THE PROBLEMS THAT COME WITH HAVING MONEY.

Ask if they believe money sometimes causes more problems than it solves. If so, what problems does it cause? Share some of the problems you see that come from having money. Ask your friends if they really enjoy the things they own or have access to. Why or why not? Be ready to explain that thanking God for the good things in your life helps you enjoy them without always wanting more.

3 :: PRESENT YOUR FRIENDS WITH THE NO-HANDFULS, ONE-HANDFUL, AND TWO-HANDFULS OPTIONS FOR FINDING CONTENTMENT.

Ask what they think is the best approach to money and life—to drop out, to work for as much as possible, or to find a way to be content with *enough*. Ask what they think *enough* is. Be ready to share what you think *enough* is and how you plan to try to live with contentment instead of constant striving to get more.

OBSERVATION EXERCISES

1. Pay attention to how many of your friends talk about wanting something or desiring money. Try to discover why they want those things, what they're willing to do to get them, and what they expect having those things will do for them. If you need to, ask a few friends some direct questions. You might be surprised how open people are about these topics.

2. Ask your parents what things they remember wanting really badly when they were your age. Did they get them? What did they have to do for them? Did they think it was worth it? What priority do they place on money and things now? Why? Ask yourself if their lives reflect their answers.

3. Pay attention to what popular songs, TV shows, movies, and magazine articles say about getting money and things this week. What are the characters willing to do for money? What does it cost them? How do their attitudes about money and things make them feel—happy, sad, frustrated? Do you think the way having money (or not having it) is shown in TV and movies reflects the truth about money? Why or why not?

4. Observe your own heart. How important are things and money to you? If you had to number the priorities in your life, what number would you give to money and possessions? Do you think your heart needs to change in this area? Why or why not?

NOT GOOD
NOT GOOD ENOUGH
ENOUGH

I'm no psychic, but I think I can predict how some of you are responding to this book so far. First of all, if you're like me, you're fascinated by Solomon's unbelievable wealth, his incredible wisdom, and his over-the-top life experiences.

Maybe you're trying to imagine what a person would do with $300 million of gold a year. Maybe you're wondering what it would be like to know more than anyone else in the world. Maybe you're trying to wrap your brain around the concept of having 1,000 sex partners. Whatever the case, you're probably amazed at the fact that Solomon was a real, historical person, and not just a fictional character.

Second, you're probably not very surprised that a man as wise as Solomon would warn us that life on this earth is meaningless. Sure, it's a depressing thought. But if you've been a Christian for a while, it's probably nothing you haven't heard before. Think about how many times you've been told that life is short. Or that nothing matters but God. Or that you shouldn't waste your time chasing parties... pleasure...sex...endless romance...or money.

Third, you're probably sharp enough to recognize that Solomon isn't trying to spoil our fun in life. Deep down, you probably already knew that the things he warns about in Ecclesiastes couldn't help you find meaning in your life. Maybe you're a little more convinced of it after digging into Ecclesiastes, but you probably already knew the difference between immediate pleasure and true, lasting satisfaction.

In other words probably nothing in this book so far has come as a great surprise to you. If that's the case, here comes a warning.

You're about to be surprised.

If you've been told by people you trust that what really matters in life is studying hard, working your tail off, accomplishing great things, becoming a successful person, developing quality relationships, and learning all you can about the world, brace yourself.

Solomon has another perspective for you to consider.

In his great experiment to find meaning in life, Solomon tried all of the good things we're encouraged to strive for by parents and guidance counselors. And his conclusion didn't change. It's all meaningless, he says.

Although he does acknowledge that some things are better than others in this short life, he's quick to point out that even the best options don't bring great satisfaction. They're just not good enough.

Solomon discovered firsthand that trying to live a successful life cannot help you find ultimate meaning.

STATUS AND POWER CAN'T SATISFY

If your place in the orchestra is second chair, what's your goal? To become first chair, right? If you get nominated to the homecoming court, you likely want to be voted homecoming queen or king. When you make the varsity basketball squad, you start thinking about when you'll crack the starting lineup...or when you'll become the leading scorer...or when you'll be named MVP.

In our culture we define success or failure in life by which direction a person is going and how far up the "ladder" he or she gets. For example, where do you rank academically in your class? What's your SAT score? What's your hotness rating? How many people in your class are more popular than you are? The higher you climb on each of those "ladders," the more successful you're considered.

Until you find yourself on the way down. You see, success is a relative thing. A person who's considered successful today may be considered a failure a year from now. Nowhere is that more obvious than in the area of popularity.

I remember the people in my high school who were super popular. Everyone knew them. Most of us envied their positions of status and power in the school. They were the top dogs. But then a strange thing happened. They went to college and found that no one there cared how popular they were in high school. All of their status was worthless.

The same thing happened after college. Some of the biggest men and women on campus became lost, directionless college grads with nothing going on in their lives. The party was over for them, and the reputations they had back in college meant nothing in the real world. Whatever meaning they thought their popularity would bring to their lives vanished.

In our society we have professional popular people called celebrities. Some of those people are famous for only one thing: being famous. People know their names only, because they hear them all the time in the media. Maybe they starred in a bootlegged sex tape on the Internet or currently have a hit song. Do you think that kind of popularity brings lasting meaning to a person's life? Me neither.

But what about those powerful and well-known people who really seem to have earned their position in the public eye? Athletes who define their sports. Actors who make us laugh and cry with their performances. Writers whose words make us think. Business leaders who shape our corporate culture. Government leaders who shape nations. The status and power enjoyed by those people must bring some meaning to life, right?

Obviously Solomon was qualified to answer that question. He was the king of Israel, after all. And he admits that it's better to be a young hot shot on the rise than an old hot shot on his way out.

But before we make a mad dash to the ladder of success and popularity, let's take a look at a story Solomon tells in Ecclesiastes 4:13-16. The story's about a kid who starts out in the streets—or perhaps even in prison—and works his way up. Eventually he grows to be more popular than the king and takes over as the leader of the kingdom himself.

It's the kind of rags-to-riches story Hollywood loves to make. Underdog defies the odds. Scratches and claws for everything he has. Catches a lucky break. Comes out on top. Lives happily ever after. Credits roll. Audience goes home feeling inspired.

But Solomon left the camera rolling, so to speak. In his story the popular young king got old. And another hot shot kid came along. The people of the kingdom decided they didn't like the old king anymore. Soon he was out of a job and the new guy was redecorating the palace.

That's how it is with popularity, status, and influence. If you have it now, you won't have it long. If you get it in the future, it will come and go quickly. If you live to be loved by lots of people you don't even know, you'll end up empty inside. Popularity and power don't give life real meaning.

ACHIEVEMENT IS TEMPORARY

Of course, not everyone is looking for popularity. Some people don't want to be famous, they just want to do something important with their lives. They want to make a difference in the world.

Solomon tried that approach too. In his search to find real meaning, the king set aside his wine, women, and song. He gave up on riches and pleasure. He said, "I'll try to do something really constructive with my life. I'll use my wealth, power, and hard work for good. Let's see if that's what really matters in life."

His first project was to build a temple for God in Jerusalem. What a way to start! As we mentioned in chapter 6, the temple Solomon constructed is considered one of the seven wonders of the ancient world. The description of it in 1 Kings 6 is incredible. The gold. The wood. The stone. The statues. Solomon spent seven years getting it all just right.

After the temple was completed, Solomon turned his attention to other advanced projects. "I built houses for myself and planted vineyards. I made gardens and parks and planted all kinds of fruit trees in them. I made reservoirs to water groves of flourishing trees" (Ecclesiastes 2:4-6).

Solomon became an architect, a builder, a gardener, a horticulturist, a scientist, an inventor, and a writer of many books, songs, and poems. He changed the landscape of Jerusalem with rich, lush gardens. He built thriving businesses that made him and his nation ridiculously wealthy. In every project he put his hand to, he enjoyed success.

And that made him happy. "My heart took delight in all my work, and this was the reward for my labor" is how he puts it in Ecclesiastes 2:10.

Solomon discovered how good it feels to see your hard work lead to success. He discovered the satisfaction that comes from finishing a project you started—and having that project turn out better than you ever imagined.

But Solomon also recognized those temporary feelings of accomplishment and pride weren't enough to make life meaningful. Look at his words in Ecclesiastes 2:11: "Yet when I surveyed all that my hands had done and what I had toiled to achieve, everything was meaningless, a chasing after the wind; nothing was gained under the sun."

Some people try to use important work and big projects as a way of making their marks on the world. They recognize how short this life is. And they sense the same things Solomon did. They say to themselves, "I'll be gone soon. Will it matter that I lived? I'd better get busy doing something significant with my life. I'd better get involved in something that will still matter after I'm gone."

That's why we hear so much talk about setting goals for ourselves and reaching for our dreams. I can still hear the mantra that played over the loudspeakers in a ride at the amusement park: "If you can imagine it, you can become it. If you can dream it, you can achieve it." And you know what? You can. But Solomon said that reaching for your dreams—and even catching them—is not good enough to give life meaning.

Don't misunderstand. There's nothing wrong with wanting to build incredible structures. Or compete in the Olympics. Or cure a disease. Or make a movie. Or help homeless people find jobs. Goals are good. But if you believe chasing your goals will make your life really matter, you're just "chasing the wind."

In the Academy Award-winning film *Million Dollar Baby*, Clint Eastwood's character agonizes over whether to help a female boxer end her life, because she's been paralyzed from the neck down and doesn't want to go on. Morgan Freeman's character helps him decide to do it by explaining that the woman had her shot at the title. She chased her dream—which is what gives meaning to life. Therefore, she now has the right to die.

What an ugly lie! Chasing your dreams will never give your life true meaning. We are deceived when we look at successful business people, sports stars, war heroes, and great leaders and think that their achievements make their lives meaningful. Solomon may have been the greatest achiever of all time, and he said those successes were good—but they did not make life worthwhile in the end.

WHY WORK?

Wait. Did you hear that? It's the sound of thousands of parents, teachers, and guidance counselors yelling, "You're not helping! How can I convince students to attempt great things in life if you tell them it won't matter in the end? Why should they work hard if it's all just meaninglessness?"

Maybe you were wondering the same thing. I know I do some days. And so did Solomon.

The fact is, there are good reasons to work hard for important things and to do your best at something no matter what it costs. But finding ultimate meaning in life isn't one of them.

Here's what will happen if you commit yourself to hard work, perseverance, and all-out effort in everything you do.

I :: YOU'LL FIND EARTHLY SATISFACTION FOR TODAY.

Solomon makes it clear that nothing in this life under the sun brings lasting meaning or full satisfaction. But he also makes it clear that our days are even more wasted when we do nothing. The only satisfaction he mentions in relation to day-to-day life under the sun is found in enjoying the results of your toil or hard work.

He's talking about the joy that comes from doing a job well. And it doesn't even matter what that job is. The late Christian singer Rich Mullins said that even something as insignificant as putting away dishes can be an act of worship, because we're imitating God's orderly nature. The work of study is tiring, but it's also a way to explore the universe God created. In the hard work of practicing music, we find joy in getting a little better all the time and recreating beauty.

He's also talking about the joy that comes from quitting time. Very few things beat the feeling of heading out to have some fun after putting in some really hard hours on a job.

Solomon leaves no doubt that work is worth doing: "Whatever your hand finds to do, do it with all your might, for in the grave, where you are going, there is neither working nor planning nor knowledge nor wisdom" (Ecclesiastes 9:10).

Whether it's schoolwork or sports training or job responsibilities, make a plan and work hard at what's in front of you. That's the best possible use of your short life. Don't expect your work to make your whole life matter. It can't do that. But it can be enough to create a sense of accomplishment today, if you'll let it.

2 :: YOU CAN EARN ETERNAL REWARDS "ABOVE THE SUN."

Keep in mind that Solomon limited his experiment to life "under the sun." You and I don't have that same restriction. Here's what Paul said to Christ's followers in Colossians 3:17: "And whatever you do, whether in word or deed, do it all in the name of the Lord Jesus, giving thanks to God the Father through him."

Whether we're studying or fixing cars or serving customers or running a country, the effort we put into our work *does* matter. Not because it will make our lives on earth more meaningful, but because we serve the God who lives above the sun. What we do *for* God matters to him—so it should matter to us too.

Instead of working for our own glory or working to feel good about how we spent our lives or working to make our bosses happy, we can work for God's glory and know that it matters forever.

Here's a question for you. Who has the more significant life's work—a medical doctor or a servant required to do lowly tasks until the day he dies? Our society would tell us the doctor's work is more meaningful, because it makes a difference in people's lives. Solomon would tell us both lives end up the same—in death. But because of Jesus, Paul tells us that the one whose life's work is more significant is the one who's working for the Lord—whatever that work may be.

Here are Paul's exact words: "Slaves, obey your earthly masters in everything; and do it, not only when their eye is on you and to win their favor, but with sincerity of heart and reverence for the Lord. Whatever you do, work at it with all your heart, as working for the Lord, not for men, since you know that you will receive an inheritance from the Lord as a reward. It is the Lord Christ you are serving" (Colossians 3:22-24).

Working for Christ's glory in any task results in eternal rewards. (We'll talk more about that in chapter 9.) That's great news for the millions of people who are locked into dull, back-breaking, or dead-end jobs. Some of us may never get a chance to lead "significant" lives or take our shot at glory. But we can be sure the work we do will have meaning if we do it for Christ.

EDUCATION IS LIMITED

We've already ticked off guidance counselors everywhere by talking about the meaninglessness of striving to reach the top of the success ladder. We might as well push them completely over the edge by talking about education itself.

Solomon warns us that if we think we're going to find ultimate meaning and purpose in education, we're wasting our time. (Those dull thuds you hear are college handbooks being thrown at my head.)

Okay, Solomon didn't put it exactly like that. In fact as you'll see in the next chapter, acquiring knowledge and wisdom can be a worthwhile thing to do with your life. But if you think being smart and knowing a lot of facts will give your life greater meaning, Solomon says you'll find yourself doing wind sprints again.

What's more, Solomon says not only will knowledge *not* unlock meaning in your life, it may end up making you unhappy in the long run. "Then I applied myself to the understanding of wisdom...but I learned that this, too, is chasing after the wind. For with much wisdom comes much sorrow; the more knowledge, the more grief" (Ecclesiastes 1:17-18).

Although gaining a better understanding of life and the world around us might sometimes make us sad, we must not avoid growing in those areas. Without that knowledge, we will miss out on a lot of what God wants to teach us. And college is a great place to gain knowledge. However, it can also be a big waste of time and money if you're there for the wrong reasons.

For example, if you're headed to college because you're ready to party with alcohol and sex and drugs, you might as well flush that application down the toilet right now. And if the only reason you're going to a school of higher learning is to make big money when you graduate, check out the last chapter again.

You're also in for a load of disappointment down the road if you think a four-year degree is going to give you the keys to the meaning of life. It won't. Ultimate meaning can't come from learning. At least it didn't work that way for the wisest guy who ever lived.

That's why he wrote, "No one can comprehend what goes on under the sun. Despite all his efforts to search it out, man cannot discover its meaning. Even if a wise man claims he knows, he cannot really comprehend it" (Ecclesiastes 8:17).

Modern research backs up his claim. In his book *A Short History of Nearly Everything,* author Bill Bryson examines what scientists currently "know" about nearly every area of the natural world. About halfway through the book, one thing becomes apparent. For all of the amazing scientific facts we tout about the world around us, we don't *know* a lot of them for certain. Every new bit of information we discover reveals more and more information that we don't know.

A good education can tell us a lot about the universe and history and math and literature, but it only just scratches the surface of what there is to be known. After four or eight or twelve years in school, all your new knowledge will have convinced you that you really don't know much. All the studying in the world will never make your life more meaningful than if you spend the rest of your days watching reruns of *That '70s Show.*

Going to college is a great plan. But don't pursue education in order to discover the meaning of life. Meaning is not available from life under the sun—even for college graduates.

HOW TO TALK TO UNBELIEVING FRIENDS ABOUT THE SEARCH FOR MEANING IN POWER, ACHIEVEMENT, AND EDUCATION

Your unbelieving friends and family members may be confused by the material in this chapter. Many people believe the only hope for a life that matters is to get a good education, do something significant, and maybe become well-known for it. They figure making a mark in the world results in a fulfilling life.

1 :: ASK YOUR FRIENDS IF THEY'VE EVER WANTED TO BE FAMOUS.

Don't be afraid to talk about your own dreams of fame. Ask your friends what they think is the real value of being famous. Ask them if they think it would be more trouble than it's worth. Talk about the idea of having people know you, love you, and remember you after you're gone. Be prepared to share Solomon's perspective that fame doesn't bring any real meaning to a person's life.

2 :: ASK YOUR FRIENDS IF THEY HAVE ANY DREAMS OR GOALS TO DO SOMETHING REALLY SIGNIFICANT WITH THEIR LIVES.

If they could accomplish any one thing in life, what would it be? Would they go for one great achievement, such as curing cancer or breaking the land speed record? Or would they prefer a whole lifetime of achievement—the kind accomplished by building a business empire or becoming a world leader or being the best ever in a chosen field? Be honest about what great work would appeal most to you. Be ready to talk about how even accomplishing that goal might still not be enough to make your short life really meaningful.

3 :: ASK YOUR FRIENDS WHAT THEY SEE AS THE POINT OF EDUCATION.

Do they plan to go to college? What do they think they'll get out of college? What do they get out of their studying in high school? Be prepared to talk about why education can't help us find ultimate meaning in life.

OBSERVATION EXERCISES

1. Who are the two or three most popular people in your school? What do you think makes them so popular? How do others treat them? Do you think they'll be popular after high school? Why or why not? Do you think popularity is making them truly happy?

2. In the media this week, pay attention to any quotations from real achievers in the worlds of sports, entertainment, politics, science, or business. See if they reveal anything about their personal level of satisfaction with life. Does it seem that success in their great projects has given them real meaning or inner peace?

3. Listen to your parents, teachers, principal, or guidance counselors talk about education and college. What do they say it will provide for you? What's the point of it, from their perspective? Do they ever talk about the limits of education?

4. Observe your own heart. If you could be wildly popular in your school or in the media, what do you think that would do for you in the long run? If you could achieve any one goal or dream you can think of, what do you imagine that would do for you? If you could instantly have all the knowledge one person can gain in four or eight years of college, what would you hope that would do for you?

THE BEST YOU CAN

THE BEST YOU CAN DO UNDER THE SUN

DO UNDER THE SUN

Here's the scenario: You've been set down in the middle of an enormous maze. The walls around you are tall and dark. The lighting is dim. Your vision is limited. You can see a little of what's in front of you and a little of what's behind you. But that's about it. Finding your way around is frustrating, to say the least. You stumble. You run into walls. But you trudge on, hoping to find a way out.

Then you spot it. A doorway with an exit sign above it. Or what looks like an exit sign. But in place of the word *Exit* is the word *Pleasure*. Through the doorway, you see what looks like a light at the end of a tunnel. *This is it!* you decide. Your way out of the maze.

Before you step through, though, you notice a sticky note stuck to the door frame. In the low light, you can barely make out the words on the note:

> To whom it may concern,
> I tried this path, but it led to a dead end.
> I'm sorry, but this isn't the way out.
> -Solomon

You're stunned, disappointed, and confused. How could it not be the way out? The path looked so promising. You debate whether to believe the note or not. Maybe Solomon didn't know what he was talking about. Maybe he missed a turn somewhere. Maybe you should try the path yourself.

Then you look around and see something you hadn't noticed before: about half a dozen other doorways just like the one in front of you. Each doorway is labeled with a sign. Education. Riches. Power. Sex. Achievement.

With a burst of excitement, you head for the nearest one. And when you get there, you find another sticky note.

> Tried it. Another dead end.
> -Solomon

So you head to the next doorway. And find another note.

> Nothing worth your time in this direction.
> -Solomon

With growing dread, you discover that every doorway has a note on it.

> Had fun in here, but then I hit the wall and had to come all the way back.
> -Solomon

> Waste of effort this way.
> -Solomon

> Don't bother!
> -Solomon

Turns out this guy, Solomon, knew his way around the maze... and had a convenient supply of sticky notes. Apparently he'd tried every passageway—and found every one to be a dead end.

So where does that leave you? On the one hand, you can be thankful that Solomon's explorations have saved you a lot of time, energy, and ultimate disappointment. On the other hand...

YOU'RE STILL STUCK IN THE MAZE!

Solomon was certainly helpful in identifying eventual dead ends. But at some point you want to say, "Stop telling me which paths *won't* take me where I want to go, and start telling me which path *will* take me there!"

FINDING MEANING IN ECCLESIASTES

Maybe a similar urge has struck you as you've explored the book of Ecclesiastes. Maybe you're ready to say, "Okay, Solomon, enough with the talk about meaninglessness. I want to hear about something that's meaningful!"

Unfortunately, there's no ultimate meaning to be found in the book of Ecclesiastes.

But don't despair. Solomon may not have had access to the passageway that brings true meaning to life. But we do. And we'll talk about that passageway, which Jesus opened when he came to our planet.

In the meantime, let's take a look at how Solomon managed to carry on despite the fact that everything he tried turned out to be meaningless. You have to admit, his experiment turned out to be pretty depressing. Nothing he tried worked for him. Yet Solomon managed to live a pretty full life anyway.

How did he do it? By focusing on the few really good things that make life pleasurable and offer temporary satisfaction, and by not expecting too much of them.

ENJOYMENT

Once Solomon understood that pleasure-seeking would never bring true meaning to his life, he was able to enjoy the good things that God provides for what they really are. You'll find Solomon's enthusiastic reviews of pleasurable activities scattered throughout the book of Ecclesiastes:

> A man can do nothing better than to eat and drink and find satisfaction in his work. This too, I see, is from the hand of God. (Ecclesiastes 2:24)

> So I saw that there is nothing better for a man than to enjoy his work, because that is his lot. (Ecclesiastes 3:22)

> Then I realized that it is good and proper for a man to eat and drink, and to find satisfaction in his toilsome labor under the sun during the few days of life God has given him—for this is his lot. Moreover, when God gives any man wealth and possessions, and enables him to enjoy them, to accept his lot and be happy in his work—this is a gift of God. (Ecclesiastes 5:18-19)

> Go, eat your food with gladness, and drink your wine with a joyful heart, for it is now that God favors what you do. (Ecclesiastes 9:7)

One thing you can do in this meaningless life under the sun is to enjoy what's good in the moment you're in. Just don't expect such enjoyment to bring ultimate meaning to your life. That's not what God intends.

FRIENDSHIPS

With all of his wisdom, Solomon recognized that the only thing worse than trying to make your way through the maze that is life on this earth...is trying to do it alone. That's why he offered the following observation about sharing yourself with someone else: "Two are better than one, because they have a good return for their work" (Ecclesiastes 4:9).

As you've probably noticed from your own experience, work is a big part of life on this earth. Not just making a living, but doing school projects and keeping things clean. Even the process of learning takes work. One advantage of friendship, then, is that when we work together, we enjoy it more and become more productive.

I was the president of my freshman class in high school, which meant I was in charge of the crew that built and decorated the freshman float for the homecoming football game. I had a great time building that float. Every day for a week everyone would come over to my house after school, and we'd work together and laugh. And when we were finished, we had a sweet-looking float to show for our efforts. The freshman class was definitely representin' at parade time.

A few days after homecoming, the guy who owned the trailer we built our float on called to tell me he needed it back. I called the people who helped build the float to ask them to help me tear it down. But every one of them was too busy to help. So I had to take apart the entire thing by myself. The job took forever, and I was miserable the entire time. That's the difference friends make.

Solomon tells us that friendship matters, because we can get more done together than we can separately. "If one falls down, his friend can help him up. But pity the man who falls and has no one to help him up!" (Ecclesiastes 4:10).

Life is hard. And everyone falls from time to time. Some falls are minor—the results of unfortunate circumstances. A flat tire. A brief illness. A bad test grade. Some falls are major. Parents splitting up. Breaking up with a long-time love. Getting in trouble with the law.

If you're alone, even a minor fall can have a major impact on your life. It can slow your momentum or bring things to a screeching halt in your life. Getting up isn't always easy.

But when you have a group of friends who care about you, they can help you to your feet again and give you the momentum you need. Later, you can return the favor when one of them falls.

You can see this principle at work when Christians get together at church. One of the main reasons the Bible instructs Christians to meet together for church is so that we can give support and encouragement to each other. Hebrews 10:25 says, "Let us not give up meeting together, as some are in the habit of doing, but let us encourage one another—and all the more as you see the Day approaching."

Solomon puts it another way: "Also, if two lie down together, they will keep warm. But how can one keep warm alone?" (Ecclesiastes 4:11).

When I was in junior high, the guys in our youth group went on a backpacking trip in California's Sierra Nevada mountains. Like a lot of junior high guys, we weren't very graceful, especially when we trudged around wearing 30-pound backpacks. While hiking with our backpacks on, we came to a stream with ice cold water. In order to cross the stream, we had to walk across a fallen log.

For reasons known only to himself, my friend Tony decided to walk backward across the log. And—surprise, surprise—he fell in. The rest of us scrambled into action as Tony was carried downstream by the current. Eventually we managed to fish him out and get him back to camp. But by that time, the damage had been done.

No matter what he did, Tony couldn't get warm. The rest of us realized that hypothermia was quickly setting in. Hypothermia is a dangerous condition. A person alone in the woods can die from it. Fortunately for Tony, our youth pastor was an Eagle Scout, and he knew what to do. He had Tony take off his wet clothes and climb into a warm sleeping bag. Then he looked at the rest of us and said, "I need one of you to strip down and get in the sleeping bag with Tony."

At first we thought he was joking. But after an awkward silence, we realized he was serious. Tony needed to borrow someone else's body heat. As Solomon might have put it, he needed someone to lie down with him to keep him warm. And guess what? It worked.

No one needs to tell you that life can be bitterly cold sometimes because of loneliness, disappointment, depression, and unkind people. But that coldness becomes a little easier to bear when you have people close to you—parents, siblings, friends— who are committed to keeping you warm.

Solomon also tells us, "Though one may be overpowered, two can defend themselves. A cord of three strands is not quickly broken" (Ecclesiastes 4:12).

This cold world is not only lonely and sad; sometimes, it's downright brutal. You'll encounter people who want to take advantage of you. You'll encounter people who want to hurt you.

What better way is there to protect yourself than to position a trusted friend at your back? Someone who can see danger com-ing your way and warn you. Someone who can stand with you against the bad guys. And if you find more than one person to watch your back—even better.

Maybe you've seen the public service announcement on TV about bullying. In the commercial, a group of grade school kids are playing at a playground. A bully approaches a small kid and threatens him. Seeing what's happening, the rest of the kids gather around, not to watch the fight, but to protect the smaller kid. They all stand together against the threat.

That's a great reason to have good friends. It's an even better reason to be part of a church. Churches are meant to be families of believers who stand together. When Christians choose instead to be loners, we're much easier for the enemy to pick us off one at a time.

Remember the movie *Gladiator*? Russell Crowe plays a slave who's used for violent sport in the arenas of ancient Rome. But he's also a former general who uses his military skills to keep himself alive. While under attack by the gladiators in one scene, he shows all of his fellow slaves how to crouch down shield-to-shield in a circle to protect themselves. The biggest and strongest slave rejects the group's strategy, because he believes he stands a better chance on his own. But he's wrong. And he gets killed. The rest of the slaves survive the attack and win the battle.

Solomon makes it clear that we all need other people. Trying to go it alone in this meaningless life only makes things harder for us—not to mention even more meaningless.

WISDOM

Solomon believed wisdom was one of the keys to a successful life. And he should have known. He had more of it than any other person who ever lived. But Solomon also understood that wisdom alone isn't enough to bring life meaning. As with enjoyment and friendship, wisdom is best when you don't expect it to be the ultimate answer.

That's why Solomon wrote, "For the wise man, like the fool, will not be long remembered; in days to come both will be forgotten. Like the fool, the wise man too must die!" (Ecclesiastes 2:16). Wisdom beats foolishness, but it's not the way out of the maze.

Many people mistake knowledge for wisdom. However, wisdom involves more than just knowing a lot of facts. Wisdom involves knowing how to apply those facts to your life and to the world around you.

Some people define wisdom as "the capacity to see life from God's perspective." In other words it's the ability to reach the right conclusion—God's conclusion—about what you observe and what you know. Solomon had the ability to look at what was going on in the world around him and understand it in the right way. That's wisdom.

Solomon tells us wisdom can and should make a real difference in how we live our lives. And he makes it clear that wisdom is always worth listening to. In Ecclesiastes 9:13-18, he describes a scenario in which a small city is surrounded and put under siege by the army of a powerful king.

His description reminds me of a scene from *The Lord of the Rings: The Return of the King*. If you saw the movie, you can probably picture the scene too. The people in the evil army of Sauron built enormous wooden structures to help them get up and over the walls of the city in which the good guys were making their stand.

Unlike the movie in which the evil army was able to storm the city, Solomon's story details how the enemy was thwarted in their attempts to overrun the city.

Solomon doesn't give us many details. Perhaps some of his earliest readers were aware of the battle he described. Here's what we do know: "Now there lived in that city a man poor but wise, and he saved the city by his wisdom" (Ecclesiastes 9:15).

The man who saved the city from almost certain doom wasn't the king. He didn't have power. He wasn't rich enough to buy his way out of danger. He was poor. He wasn't a mighty warrior who could fight his way through trouble. All he had was wisdom. And he used it to save the city.

That's why Solomon concluded, "Wisdom is better than strength" (Ecclesiastes 9:16). That's also why he said, "The quiet words of the wise are more to be heeded than the shouts of a ruler of fools. Wisdom is better than weapons of war" (Ecclesiastes 9:17-18).

You'll probably never find yourself in a city besieged by war. But you will have plenty of opportunities to use wisdom to get yourself—and others—out of tight spots. Remember, life is full of sneak attacks and hidden traps—dangers that can be avoided or defeated with a little wisdom.

For example, Solomon tells us, "A good name is better than fine perfume" (Ecclesiastes 7:1). In the book of Proverbs, he says, "A good name is more desirable than great riches" (Proverbs 22:1). He's talking about reputation. Based on his wise observations of life, Solomon concluded that a good reputation is worth more than anything money can buy.

We all know people who have foolishly sacrificed their good names to get something the easy way. Maybe they told lies to get out of trouble and earned the reputation of people who can't be trusted. Maybe they went too far in physical relationships in order to become popular and picked up reputations for being immoral or easy. Maybe they didn't always give their best efforts when they worked and got reputations for being lazy.

My dad is an architect, and he's known as a man of integrity. He has a good reputation, one that he's earned. He's made wise choices throughout his life to protect his reputation. Recently these choices paid off big time for him. A client falsely accused him of incompetence on a building project. Due to those accusations, my dad lost the project and was sued by the company that hired him to do the job.

However, because my dad has always taken careful steps to do everything with integrity, two things happened. First, people who knew my dad came to his defense. They knew the accusation didn't match his reputation, and they said so. Second, based on his good work records, my dad was able to make his case that he had done everything right. And he won the case. His good name protected him when attacks came. That's wise living.

That's just one example of wisdom in action. I could fill another book with hundreds of other examples. But it will be far better for you to grow in wisdom yourself than to read examples of others living wisely.

So how can you get wise? Here are three strategies straight from God's Word:

I :: ASK FOR WISDOM.

In the New Testament, James tells us we can follow Solomon's example by just asking God for wisdom: "If any of you lacks wisdom, he should ask God, who gives generously to all without finding fault, and it will be given to him" (James 1:5).

Did you catch that part about "without finding fault"? It doesn't matter if you've made a lot of unwise choices in the past. It doesn't matter if you're poor...or if you don't consider yourself very smart...or if you feel really lost. God doesn't sort through the applications of people looking for wisdom, disqualifying candidates he doesn't consider worthy of his help. He gives wisdom to everyone who asks—and who believes he will deliver it.

2 :: SEARCH FOR WISDOM.

As you've seen throughout this book, Solomon described most of the results of his big Ecclesiastes experiment as nothing more than "chasing the wind." But one project he says is worth our while is the search for wisdom.

Look at his words in Proverbs 2:1-6:

> My son, if you accept my words, and store up my commands within you, turning your ear to wisdom and applying your heart to understanding, and if you call out for insight and cry aloud for understanding, and if you look for it as for silver and search for it as for hidden treasure, then you will understand the fear of the Lord and find the knowledge of God. For the Lord gives wisdom.

Notice all of the actions called for in that passage. *Turn your ear. Apply your heart. Call out. Cry aloud. Look for it. Search for it.* Looking for wisdom is something you *do*. It requires effort on your part. And if you're willing to put the effort into your search, you'll find success. You'll find wisdom.

If you're looking for a place to start, try reading the books of Proverbs and James. They're packed full of God's perspective on real-life issues such as money, friendship, emotions, and conflict. If you stuff those writings into your cranium, you'll begin to think like a wise guy—or a wise girl. Knowing God's perspective will help you see the world in the right way and come to the right conclusions about what you observe.

3 :: LISTEN TO WISE PEOPLE.

When you start digging into Solomon's book of Proverbs, you'll notice something right away: Wise people know how to listen and take advice from wiser people.

> Listen, my son, to your father's instruction and do not forsake your mother's teaching. (Proverbs 1:8)

> Plans fail for lack of counsel, but with many advisers they succeed. (Proverbs 15:22)

> A rebuke impresses a man of discernment more than a hundred lashes a fool. (Proverbs 17:10)

That last one is a biggie. In your search for wisdom, you're going to find out that you've been wrong about some things. You're going to make some mistakes and get "rebuked." A fool will respond by saying, "I'm not wrong!"—no matter how much he gets corrected or punished. A wise person, on the other hand, will be humble enough to ask himself, "Am I wrong here? What could I have done better? How can I learn from this?"

God has placed some wise people in your life—including your parents. Listening to them is a great way to gather wisdom.

THINKING BEYOND THE MAZE

Your life on this earth will be a whole lot better if you take Solomon's advice about learning to enjoy the moment, attaching yourself to friends, and becoming a wisdom hunter. But you won't find ultimate meaning in any of those things.

Remember, Solomon conducted his experiment in order to find the meaning of life, a real point to his existence. And though he didn't find anything "under the sun" to fulfill his deepest needs, he did find something beyond the sun. In the next two chapters, we're going to discover what he found. We'll find out how we can live for something that *really* matters—both in this life and in the next one.

HOW TO TALK TO UNBELIEVING FRIENDS ABOUT THE BEST YOU CAN DO "UNDER THE SUN"

Even philosophers who leave God out of their thinking talk about the best possible way to live in a difficult world. Your unbelieving friends and family may have thought about it too. If a conversation allows for it, see if their observations of life line up with Solomon's.

1 :: ASK YOUR FRIENDS HOW THEY THINK A PERSON CAN HAVE THE BEST LIFE ON EARTH.

Do they think it requires riches...love...accomplishments...or some combination of those? Pay attention to whether they mention any of the three topics covered in this chapter: enjoyment, friendship, and wise living. How do your friends plan to make the best life they can for themselves? What do they think it will do for them?

2 :: ASK YOUR FRIENDS IF THEY REALLY ENJOY GOOD THINGS IN LIFE.

Do they believe enjoying life is a decision a person makes or is it something that happens as a result of circumstances? Ask them what keeps people from really enjoying good moments. Talk about how expectations play into the idea of enjoying life. Be prepared to talk about how you try to enjoy good things in life as gifts from God for the moment.

3 :: ASK YOUR FRIENDS WHAT FRIENDSHIP IS WORTH.

Do they enjoy having a lot of friends, a few close friends, or being alone? Ask them what they think people gain by having friends instead of doing everything on their own. Be ready to talk about the things Solomon said come with having a good friend. Ask your friends if they've seen the same things in their own lives.

4 :: ASK YOUR FRIENDS IF THEY BELIEVE IN WISDOM.

An interesting question to ask unbelievers is what they think about wisdom. Where does it come from? What's it good for? How do you get it? Be ready to share your understanding that wisdom is the ability to come to the right conclusions about what you see in life. Explain that Christians believe that since God designed the world and knows everything, he's the best place to find the right ideas about life. In other words, wisdom naturally comes from him.

OBSERVATION EXERCISES

1. Pay attention to the people in your life who really seem to be enjoying themselves. Not just people doing fun things or pretending to have a good time, but those who are clearly enjoying the moments they're given. What do you think makes them able to do that? Do they have anything in common with each other? Are Christians any better at finding joy in the moments of life than unbelievers—or vice versa?

2. Pay attention to what the media says about friendship this week. Do any of the movies or TV shows you watch reflect Solomon's teaching that friends help you make the most of the life you're given? Do any stories suggest that it's better to be a loner? What are some of the benefits you see of having friends as depicted in the media?

3. Who are two or three of the wisest people you know? Why do they seem wise to you? How do those people differ from others in their choices...their responses to conflict...the words they say... or the way they respond to people in authority?

4. Observe your own heart. If you had the ability to enjoy the moments of your life as God's gifts, and if you had some really close friends, and if you had lots of wisdom—would that be enough to make life meaningful for you? Why or why not?

TIME WILL
TIME WILL TELL
TELL

I grew up in Southern California, where the weather conditions tend to be pretty consistent. Occasionally the area gets a rainstorm. But most of the time, you'll hear the TV weather person say something like this: "Sunny today, with highs in the 70s." People joke that being a weather forecaster in Los Angeles is the easiest job in television news.

Since moving to Texas, I've learned that's not the way the weather works in other places. Here, and in many parts of the world, the locals like to say, "Don't like the weather? Wait five minutes and it'll change." A beautiful sunny day in the Midwest can unexpectedly turn cold and stormy. A blizzard in the mountains can quickly yield to perfect picnic weather and then switch back again in the same afternoon. Those are the places that keep weather forecasters in business.

As Solomon was conducting his great experiment, he jotted down some observations about time. And the conclusion he reached about our days on earth could apply to the weather in Texas during the spring: *Things are always changing.*

THE SECRET OF TIME

Whether you're a fool or a wise guy, rich or on welfare, the president of a country or just the king of your own locker, you're going to die. Just like everyone else. You might get 70, 80, 90, or 100 years on this earth, but eventually your time will run out.

So you're left with the responsibility of making the most of the time you have. In order to do that, though, you have to understand the nature of time on this earth. The fact that the way things are right now isn't the way things will be tomorrow. Or even an hour from now.

Things change. Times change. And there's not much we can do to control that. Our times are not up to us. To paraphrase my Texas friends: Don't like the time you're in? Wait five minutes, and it'll change.

In Ecclesiastes 3:1-8, Solomon describes the chameleon-like nature of our time on earth in a poem about the changing seasons of life.

> There is a time for everything,
> and a season for every activity under heaven:
> a time to be born and a time to die,
> a time to plant and a time to uproot,
> a time to kill and a time to heal,
> a time to tear down and a time to build,
> a time to weep and a time to laugh,
> a time to mourn and a time to dance,
> a time to scatter stones and a time to gather them,
> a time to embrace and a time to refrain,
> a time to search and a time to give up,
> a time to keep and a time to throw away,
> a time to tear and a time to mend,
> a time to be silent and a time to speak,
> a time to love and a time to hate,

a time for war and a time for peace.

You'll notice that many of the "times" on Solomon's list are beyond our control. None of us had any say in when we were born. And most of us will have little say in when we die. Likewise, farmers are at the mercy of nature when it comes to planting and harvesting (or uprooting).

Solomon's father, David, lived in a time of killing and war. God had asked David to wipe out Israel's enemies. And for the most part, David did—killing thousands upon thousands. In return God kept his promise to King David that his son Solomon's reign would be a time of healing and peace for Israel.

Chances are you've noticed dozens of times of destruction and construction. Near my house, contractors recently tore down an old Burger King restaurant that had stood for years. The place was falling apart and getting ugly—so the time came to knock it to the ground. And then the time came to build a new Burger King in its place.

Solomon warns us that everyone will experience times of weeping and mourning. Loved ones die. Bad things happen. And we have no control over any of it. If you live long enough, you can be sure that you will experience times of great sadness and grieving. Welcome to life under the sun.

On the other hand, you'll also experience your share of unbelievably happy times. Times to laugh. Times to dance (unless you don't move that way). Times to hang out with good friends. Times to date and marry someone you love. Times to enjoy your kids. Times to enjoy your grandkids. They're all part of the package of life under the sun.

When Solomon uses the word *embrace* in Ecclesiastes 3:5, he's talking about sex—the kind that occurs between a husband

and a wife. If you're not married, God says you should be in a time of refraining. But to married people, God says clearly: it's time to get busy with your spouse (1 Corinthians 7:3-5).

Solomon also wants us to recognize there are times to hold on to things—including hope that we'll find what we're searching for. But there also come times to quit searching for things we've lost and times to throw away things we don't need any more. In other words there's a time to buy and a time to sell what you bought .

We also go through seasons of love and hate. You can find any number of verses about love in the Bible—including one that says, "God is love" (1 John 4:16). As Christians, we're called to love him with everything we've got. We're also instructed to love our neighbors as deeply as we love ourselves. So in a sense, it's always time for us to love. But we're also called to imitate the God we love by hating what he hates (Psalm 97:10). If you're curious about what God could possibly hate, check out the list in Proverbs 6:16-19.

Solomon was as frustrated as we are about being at the mercy of time (Ecclesiastes 3:10). But in his wisdom, he uncovered some truths about time that can help us develop a healthy perspective toward the seasons of our lives.

I :: TIME IS GOD'S CANVAS.

God is not limited to time as we are. He doesn't live in minutes and seconds and hours. He exists outside of time in *eternity* (a word that actually means "outside of time").

However, God did create time—and he controls it. Obviously many things that happen within the realm of time are not good. But God makes good use of every event for his purposes. I love the way Solomon puts it in Ecclesiastes 3:11: "He has made everything beautiful in its time." Solomon shows us that on the canvas of history, there are no missed brush strokes or ugly spots. Somehow God takes all of it and makes it...art. He uses every moment in time for his beautiful purposes.

2 :: WE FEEL THE PULL OF TIMELESSNESS.

Part of our burden in life is that we are trapped in time. I can't make that clock move to the end of a bad Monday, no matter how hard I try. And I can't stop the minutes from flying by when I'm loving my day off. Whether times are good or bad, we have to keep plugging away. That's part of life under the sun. But we know deep inside there's another way.

Solomon tells us God has "set eternity in the hearts of men" (Ecclesiastes 3:11). He's hardwired us with a longing to step beyond the walls of time and be free. He's built into us a desire to be with him in the timelessness of heaven. It's something we feel deep inside, but it's not something we can fully understand on our own. It begins to make sense only when we see this longing in the light of the story of Jesus.

One of the most fascinating men I've ever met is a missionary and writer named Don Richardson. He came to talk at our church when I was a kid, and then he stayed at our house. He told us exciting stories from his travels around the world, many of which are collected in his book *Eternity in their Hearts: Startling Evidence of Belief in the One True God in Hundreds of Cultures Throughout the World.*

In the book Richardson describes real-life encounters between missionaries and members of tribes who had never heard of traditional Christianity. The missionaries were amazed to discover that members of every tribe already had some belief in the one true God—before they encountered anyone from the outside world. Just as Solomon described, God had placed some deep knowledge of himself in their hearts. What they needed was outside help to make sense of their belief. They needed someone to tell them the story of Jesus.

3 :: WE MUST LIVE NOW.

It's true that we'll experience many different "times" in our lives. And it's true that we're built for eternity with God. However, we need to understand that this moment—*right now*—is our gift from God. Therefore, we have a responsibility to live this—and every moment as if it matters. Enjoy it as a present. Take it seriously. The fact that it may not be the kind of moment we would have chosen for ourselves shouldn't make a difference. It's a moment God's given us. And we should treat it that way (Ecclesiastes 3:12-13).

WHERE IS JUSTICE?

Peter Parker wanted out of the superhero game. He decided the responsibility was too much to bear. The lifestyle was too crazy to maintain. His duties kept him from living the life he wanted to live.

So why did audiences cheer during *Spider Man 2* when he put his tights back on? For one thing most of us agree with the notion that "With great power comes great responsibility." We respect people who set aside personal desires in order to do the right thing.

But we also cheered, because we're hungry for justice. If someone has the power to save innocent people and make bad guys pay for their crimes, we root for that person. As with our longing for eternity, God has hard-wired us with a longing to see good people rewarded and evil people defeated. That's why shows such as *CSI* and *Law & Order* are so popular. They show us bad people doing bad things. Then they show those bad people getting caught, convicted, and punished.

Sometimes, though, real life doesn't work out as well as a TV drama.

Solomon recognized that justice isn't always served right away. Look at his words in Ecclesiastes 4:1-3:

> Again I looked and saw all the oppression that was taking place under the sun:
>
> I saw the tears of the oppressed—
>   and they have no comforter;
> power was on the side of their oppressors—
>   and they have no comforter.
> And I declared that the dead,
>   who had already died,
> are happier than the living,
>   who are still alive.
> But better than both
>   is he who has not yet been,
> who has not seen the evil
>   that is done under the sun.

Solomon saw real evil being done to the innocent. He saw that the men who committed the evil deeds had power enough to escape prosecution. In other words they appeared to get away with their crimes. And Solomon concluded that it was better to be dead—or never to have been born at all—than to see that kind of injustice and evil.

Who hasn't felt that way at some time or another? The NBC news program *Dateline* did a story on the sex trade in Thailand. In the story they introduced us to children—cute little girls as young as five years old—who had been kidnapped or sold into slavery as prostitutes and trained in sexual acts they never should have understood. Then the story introduced a doctor from the United States who didn't know he was on camera as he talked about the things he paid to have the young prostitutes do for him.

Depending on your personality, seeing that kind of evil probably makes you either angry or sick—or both. And it probably makes you long for justice. That *Dateline* story focused on an American group that was founded because of that same longing for justice. The International Justice Mission uses lawyers and former military and intelligence professionals in attempts to rescue people from abuse, forced prostitution, and slavery. Their motto is simple: Seek justice.

But even a thousand inspiring groups of heroes, such as those at the International Justice Mission, could not stop all the injustice in the world. Even the powerful King Solomon couldn't stop women and children from being oppressed by evil people.

That reality makes some people question the reality of an all-powerful God who exists outside of time. Think about how many times you've heard someone ask a question like this: *How could a loving, powerful, and good God allow such evil and suffering to exist in the world? Shouldn't he be held to the same standard that Peter Parker lives by: "With great power comes great responsibility"?*

In answering those questions, Solomon makes it clear that the God who exists outside of time and "above the sun" pays careful attention to what goes on in our world. And while he will not keep people from choosing wickedness, he will "call the past to account" (Ecclesiastes 3:15). He will execute justice—in his time. "God will bring to judgment both the righteous and the wicked, for there will be a time for every activity, a time for every deed" (Ecclesiastes 3:17). And he'll do it better than we could ever hope to do it ourselves.

As the highest official in his country, Solomon was all too aware that human justice systems fail. Sometimes we can't catch the bad guys. Sometimes we can't convict them. Sometimes a corrupt system protects them, instead of punishing them. Solomon said he saw "wickedness" in his own places of justice and judgment—places that should have been full of goodness (Ecclesiastes 3:16).

Many people believe America might have the best system of justice in the world. But even the American justice system fails—perhaps more often than any of us would care to know. Guilty men often go free. DNA testing suggests that we've locked up many innocent people. And the O. J. Simpson trial proved that we just flat get it wrong sometimes.

I don't know whether O. J. was guilty or innocent of killing his wife and Ron Goldman. Either way, the justice system failed. Either he did it, and the criminal courts declared him "not guilty," or he didn't do it, and the civil courts declared him "guilty." One way or the other, justice failed in his case.

Unfortunately humans are not superheroes. We don't know how to bring justice on evil. Solomon said that makes us similar to animals. That is we're certainly closer to animals than we are to God. We live. We die. We're buried. We decay. We've got a lot in common with the soulless beasts. "Who knows if the spirit of man rises upward and if the spirit of the animal goes down into the earth?" (Ecclesiastes 3:21)

Unbelievers sometimes wrongly point to that verse as evidence that Solomon didn't believe in the afterlife. But we know that's not true. In Ecclesiastes 3 alone, he tells us that God puts eternity in human hearts and that God will judge us. Solomon knew eternity exists. His point here is that we can't see it happening "under the sun." All we see with our eyes is that a dead human and a dead dog have a lot in common. And one of those things is that neither is very good at delivering true justice.

Finally, Solomon throws up his hands and says a person might as well enjoy the moment in front of him, because "who can bring him to see what will happen after him?" (Ecclesiastes 3:22). But guess what? About a thousand years after Solomon died, God did exactly that.

EYEWITNESS TO ETERNITY

The apostle John was called "the disciple Jesus loved." He might have been Jesus' best friend during his years on earth. John turned out to be the guy Solomon imagined when he wrote "who can bring him to see what will happen after him?" The answer was God, who brought John to see what's on the other side of sun after the clock stops ticking.

John wrote what he saw in the book of Revelation. And his book is the reason we know Solomon was right. God *will* bring justice on all who deserve it. No evil will go unpunished. Everyone will have to give an account of his or her actions.

Humans might be bad at delivering a fair judgment, but God isn't. God gets it exactly right. Let's look at John's eyewitness account of God's judgment from Revelation 20:11-15:

> Then I saw a great white throne and him who was seated on it. Earth and sky fled from his presence, and there was no place for them. (Revelation 20:11)

Solomon would have appreciated this picture. If you remember he had a pretty impressive throne room himself, by earthly standards. We learned in 1 Kings 10 that Solomon's throne of ivory and gold was the most impressive seat on earth. Compared to the throne of God, though, Solomon's would have been as impressive as a beanbag chair.

But in John's description, it is not the throne that's intimidating. It's the occupant. No one will want to make eye contact with the One sitting on the throne. Even the earth and sky will look for a place to hide. But there will be no way out. The time of judgment will have come, just as Solomon promised it would.

> And I saw the dead, great and small, standing before the throne, and books were opened. Another book was opened, which is the book of life. The dead were judged according to what they had done as recorded in the books. The sea gave up the dead that were in it, and death and Hades gave up the dead that were in them, and each person was judged according to what he had done. (Revelation 20:12-13)

What John saw in that place must have been staggering. Imagine billions of people assembled in one place—waiting to be judged once and for all according to God's holy standard. The small and the great gathered together. Peasants and criminals, shoulder-to-shoulder, before God's final judgment with kings, presidents, and billionaires. People whose bodies ended up in watery ocean graves, their names forgotten, next to men and women whose massive funerals were witnessed by thousands.

Some of the wealthiest people the world has ever known will stand before God with no chance to buy their way out of judgment. They'll find out that credit cards aren't going to work after all.

Bible scholars disagree about whether the dead people assembled in this passage include everyone who has ever lived or only those who have not placed their trust in Christ for salvation. Either way, the method of judgment is the same.

First, books are opened that list every action a person has taken in his or her life. Good or bad. If you've taken accounting, you might imagine these books as accounting ledgers. They list what each person "owes" to God for choices they made to reject his will.

God is absolutely pure and holy. If you're into physics, you can think of him as matter and sin as anti-matter. The two substances cannot occupy the same space together. If any sin exists within a person, he or she cannot be with God. Period.

The one thing we know for sure about God's judgment is that no one will face it with a clean record. The apostle Paul tells us "all have sinned and fall short of the glory of God" (Romans 3:23). What's more, the price that God demands as punishment for sin is brutally expensive: "For the wages of sin is death" (Romans 6:23).

Your name will be read. The books of your life will be opened. And all of your offenses—the times when you chose to do things your own way instead of God's way—will be revealed. Your excuses will melt away into one word: guilty. Your guilt will be obvious before the Judge. And then the price for your offenses will be read: blood and death.

This description may read like a script for a creepy, gothic, horror movie—but that's what sin requires. The writer of Hebrews explained that without the shedding of blood, there can't be any forgiveness of sins (see Hebrews 9:22). The only thing that works is death. Even an animal sacrifice won't cut it at this judgment. Either you'll have to pay for your sin with your own eternal death (hell that is)—or someone has to pay the price for you. Someone without his own sin to pay for.

Remember that angry desire for God to bring justice on evildoers? What happens to it when you picture yourself stand-

ing before God? We all want the wicked to pay for their sins...
until we realize the wicked includes us. We're as guilty as anyone, because we've all chosen to violate God's instructions. We've
offended his purity. The book of Romans makes it clear that no
one is righteous enough on his or her own to be with God in
heaven. Not you. Not me. When I consider that, I feel like lower-
ing my "Justice Now" sign just a little.

> Then death and Hades were thrown into the lake of fire.
> The lake of fire is the second death. If anyone's name was
> not found written in the book of life, he was thrown into
> the lake of fire. (Revelation 20:14-15)

People who are condemned by their own works have one final
hope. At God's judgment seat, another book is opened. This one
is called the Book of Life. In it are the names of all who made a
crucial decision at some point in their lives. People who recognized they were doomed to be apart from God forever, because
of their sinfulness. People who made the choice to put all of their
hope and trust in the only One who can pay the price they owe—
Jesus Christ, God's own Son. People who believed that he came
to earth as a man...lived a perfect life...gave his life to pay for the
sins of all humankind...and conquered death by rising from the
dead. People who made the choice to trust him personally. In
other words people who were saved by their faith in the Son.

Understand something important here: None of the people
listed in the Book of Life did anything to earn a spot inside. Their
names are written in the book as a gift from God, because Jesus
paid what they owed. Period. (Ephesians 2:8-9) He paid for all
their sins with his own blood, his own life. For free. And each of
them accepted that gift and will be welcomed into the kingdom
of heaven.

And what about the people whose names aren't found in the
Book of Life? They made their choice during their days "under

the sun" to reject Jesus' offer. That leaves only one destination for them—the one apart from God. The one John described as a "lake of fire."

A TIME FOR JUDGMENT

So where does that leave searchers like us? We know from Solomon's repeated warnings that we won't find anything apart from God that really makes life worth living. We may be able to do some things to make life easier, but none of them will take away the emptiness we all carry around with us.

But we also know we carry something else in our hearts. That is the nagging realization that something meaningful lies beyond this world. We know eternity exists. Even atheists and agnostics, who refuse to believe anything they can't see with their eyes, feel forever's pull. They long for eternity even if they can't bring themselves to hope in it.

Solomon had the courage to be brutally honest at every stage of his search for meaning, including admitting that the ultimate answer must lie beyond what he could see and experience.

Observation can tell us a lot about the world and the God who created it. But observation has limits. Eventually each of us has to decide what we will believe about the things we can't see on this side of the sun.

A girl named Daisha made her decision at one of the Planet Wisdom Student Conferences we conduct around the country. Some years later, I received this e-mail, from Daisha's youth pastor, at a camp where I was teaching about Solomon's search in Ecclesiastes:

Mark,

I just want to drop you a quick note regarding one of our students. Sunday morning during Sunday school, I received a call from one of our youth sponsors telling me her 17-year-old sister was killed in a car accident. This girl was one of our key kids. She was going to be a senior in high school, on student council, captain of the cheerleading squad, and in love with Jesus. Obviously this is a very difficult week for us. The reason I am e-mailing you is because several years ago, this young lady accepted Christ at one of your conferences. Yesterday, the student council organized an impromptu vigil at the crash site. They called me and asked me if I would be willing to share. I shared with the kids not to worry about Daisha, because I knew for certain that when she left this earth, she stepped into the arms of Jesus. I cannot imagine going through an experience like this without having that knowledge.

After reading the message, I felt sad for Daisha's family and friends. But I'm not telling you her story because I want to manipulate you with strong emotions about death. Instead, I want to persuade you to think about the cold, hard reality of our short, short lives. If Daisha had lived to 96 instead of 16, we wouldn't call it tragic. But the reality would be the same when it came time for the judgment. The only question that really matters is this: Is her name written in the Book of Life. Daisha's name is there. Is yours?

If so we're going to see in the next chapter that your choice to trust in Jesus makes all the difference in the universe as to whether your life is meaningless or whether it will count for something after it comes to an end.

HOW TO TALK TO UNBELIEVING FRIENDS ABOUT TIME AND JUDGMENT

The issues in this chapter might be the most important ones in this book when it comes to sharing with your unbelieving friends and family. Ask God to give you opportunities to talk to your friends about these issues and the ability to share honestly and accurately what you believe.

1 :: ASK YOUR FRIENDS ABOUT THE TIMES OF THEIR LIVES.

Bring up Solomon's poem in Ecclesiastes 3:1-8, which is popular with both Christians and unbelievers for its perspective on life. Ask your friends how they would describe the best time in their lives...and the worst time. Ask them how they would describe the time of life they're in right now. Be prepared to answer the same questions about your life. Ask your friends if they ever feel resentful, because they can't control the times of their lives.

If your friends are open to talking about Ecclesiastes 3:1-8, read them verse 11 too. Ask if they believe everything is beautiful in its time. Do they believe in God enough to buy into the idea that each of us carries the notion of eternity in our hearts? If they believe in eternity, what do they expect from it? Be ready to share your beliefs as well.

2 :: ASK YOUR FRIENDS ABOUT JUSTICE.

Have your friends ever been frustrated by the fact that evil seems to win in this world? Or by the fact that justice isn't delivered? Or by the fact that the innocent aren't protected? Be ready to talk about God's involvement in human activities and the issue of human freedom to make wrong choices. Ask your friends what they think about the idea of a final judgment. Do they believe we all will eventually be held responsible for our actions? Be prepared to explain what you believe.

3 :: ASK YOUR FRIENDS ABOUT THEIR STANDARDS OF JUSTICE.

Ask them if they believe in heaven. And if so what should be the standard for getting in? Ask them what they believe is a good enough reason for God to keep someone out of heaven. Ask them if they believe anyone should be sent to hell. Ask them what they think of the idea of perfection and sinlessness being the standard for getting into heaven. Be ready to explain your understanding of the good news—that nobody can make it into heaven because the standard is impossibly high. And that Jesus paid for all of our sin in order to make it possible for us to get to heaven...if we'll believe and accept God's gift.

OBSERVATION EXERCISES

1. Pay attention to the people in and around your life. Measure them against Solomon's poem about time. Do you see anyone who's in the time to be born...or the time to weep...or the time to laugh...or the time to refrain from embracing...or the time to go to war...or the time to be silent? Check out the rest of Solomon's list. How does a person's season of life seem to impact his or her emotions, activities, and responses to God?

2. Pay attention to the TV shows and movies you watch this week. What characters are motivated by a desire for justice? What makes those characters qualified to seek justice against people who do wrong? How do they seek justice? What do their attempts at righting wrongs accomplish? Are you drawn to stories that deal with getting justice for the oppressed—and against bad guys?

3. If you have any pets, keep an eye on them for a few days. How are humans like animals? How are we different? What are your observations? Do you see any observable clues that we are eternal beings and animals are not? If so what did you find? If not what do you make of that?

4. Observe your own heart. Are you absolutely convinced that your name is written in the Book of Life? If so why? If not why aren't you? Who could you talk to in order to make absolutely sure you understand the issues involved in choosing to trust in the Son for your eternal salvation?

A LIFE THAT

A LIFE THAT MATTERS

MATTERS

So where does that leave you?

You've waded through nine chapters of failed experiments. You've developed a working knowledge of all the things that *can't* bring ultimate meaning to life. You've watched Solomon try one dead-end path after another in his search for fulfillment. Money. Sex. Alcohol. Laughter. Romance. Achievement. Power. Popularity. Education. You've learned the difference between temporary pleasures and long-lasting satisfaction.

You've read Solomon's thoughts regarding the emptiness he felt. And the meaninglessness he saw all around him. And the groaning of his heart to find something to live for.

Now what?

Solomon has come to the final chapter of Ecclesiastes. He's also come to the final chapter of his life. He's done everything he's going to do. He's learned everything he will ever know. He's finished his Great Experiment.

All that's left is the final report. But what's left to say? Is meaninglessness the only thing we can expect in this life? Will Solomon's book of Ecclesiastes end with a depressing conclusion for all meaning-seekers? Or will Solomon drop some last-minute pearls of wisdom on us to give us some direction in finding ultimate meaning?

Read on....

NO HOPE WITHOUT GOD

Solomon wraps up the book of Ecclesiastes with three nuggets of advice. Together they reveal an important truth. That is nothing on this earth—apart from God—will give your life meaning. Nothing you can buy, experience, or learn will ever take away the groaning in your heart. Ultimate meaning can only be found "above the sun."

Therefore, the person searching for ultimate meaning would be wise to pay attention to Solomon's advice.

1 :: "REMEMBER YOUR CREATOR IN THE DAYS OF YOUR YOUTH" (ECCLESIASTES 12:1).

Solomon points out that since the answers we're all looking for have something to do with God, we shouldn't wait to pay attention to him. In fact a wise strategy would be to start an intimate relationship with him immediately.

I've met plenty of students who seem to have decided on just the opposite plan. They assume they'll have plenty of time to figure out what to do about God when they're older. But for the time being, they want to have fun. They want to explore for themselves the things Solomon has already tried. They want to experience life.

Solomon recognized the appeal of that approach to life. Look at his words in Ecclesiastes 11:9: "Be happy, young man, while you are young, and let your heart give you joy in the days of your youth. Follow the ways of your heart and whatever your eyes see."

But that's not the end of the verse. You see, Solomon, with his incredible wisdom, realized the danger in that approach to life. That's why he ends the verse with a warning: "but know that for all these things God will bring you to judgment."

If you choose to follow the paths Solomon tried, three things will happen. One, you'll find nothing but dead ends. Two, God will be displeased that you ignored the warnings in his Word. And three, you'll become a victim of the aging process.

Using poetic language, Solomon gives us the details of that process in Ecclesiastes 12:1-7. Look at the images he uses to describe our deterioration:

- "the sun and the light and the moon and the stars grow dark, and the clouds return after the rain" (Ecclesiastes 12:2). Your whole body will lose energy and vitality.

- "when the keepers of the house tremble, and the strong men stoop" (Ecclesiastes 12:3). Your arms and legs will become weak and feeble.

- "when the grinders cease because they are few" (Ecclesiastes 12:3). Your teeth may give you trouble and fall out, making it harder to eat.

- "and those looking through the windows grow dim" (Ecclesiastes 12:3). Your eyes will get weaker, and your vision will blur.

- "when men rise up at the sound of birds" (Ecclesiastes 12:4). Just like the older folks you know, you won't be able to sleep late.

- "but all their songs grow faint" (Ecclesiastes 12:4). Your hearing will decline.

- "when men are afraid of heights and of dangers in the streets" (Ecclesiastes 12:5). You'll get timid and start to worry about bad things that might happen.

- "when the almond tree blossoms" (Ecclesiastes 12:5). Whatever hair you have left will turn white.

- "and the grasshopper drags himself along" (Ecclesiastes 12:5). Like a grasshopper with one leg, you'll move slowly instead of darting around as you do now.

- "and desire is no longer stirred." (Ecclesiastes 12:5). You'll lose interest in sex, exercise, food, and drinking. That's when you'll know you're close to the end.

Not the prettiest picture in the world, is it? Solomon points out that everyone who lives long enough eventually reaches this stage of life. And that's not the time to start remembering God! You'll have wasted the best years of your life! Solomon urges his readers—especially the young ones—not to wait until they're half-dead to start living for God. Because that's just...let's all say it together...meaningless.

2 :: "FEAR GOD" (ECCLESIASTES 12:13).

One way to remember God when you're young is to develop a healthy fear of him. Not a horror-movie kind of fear. Not a please-don't-strike-me-dead kind of fear. But a deep respect for who he is, what he's done, and what he's capable of. In other words Solomon is saying, "Respect God as he should be respected."

In Ecclesiastes 5:1-7, Solomon warns people about making foolish vows or promises to God and then not keeping them. We don't make a lot of formal vows to God these days, but it was a common part of worship in Solomon's time. Some foolish people made vows to God and didn't follow through with them. Solomon helped them see that breaking a promise to God is *always* a bad idea.

A similar mistake that many people make today is to treat God too casually. Many believers try to interact with God as though he's one of us—or maybe just a little more important than us. That doesn't work. The poet-king wrote, "Do not be quick with your mouth, do not be hasty in your heart to utter anything before God. God is in heaven and you are on earth, so let your words be few" (Ecclesiastes 5:2). In other words think about who you're dealing with.

God exists in eternity in heaven. We are trapped in time and space on this sin-ridden earth. God is our Creator. We are his creation. He owes us nothing. We owe him everything. To say we rank infinitely lower on the VIP list than he does is an understatement. Realistically speaking, we're not even worthy to be mentioned in the same breath as God. No wonder Solomon says, "Therefore stand in awe of God" (Ecclesiastes 5:7).

Some people may point out that we live in a different era than Solomon. We enjoy a closer relationship with God than he did. Because Jesus came and paid the penalty for our sin, those who trust in him are forgiven. We can know we are loved and forgiven by God. Jesus said we can call God "Daddy." The book of Hebrews says we can approach God with confidence, knowing he listens and responds to us.

And all those things are true.

However, too many of us turn confidence in our relationship with God into casualness toward him. Instead of approaching God in prayer with boldness, we approach him with disrespectful hearts. We demand things from him. We forget to thank him for all the good gifts and moments he drops into our lives. We disrespect him. We fail to fear him. We forget that he is the Creator and we are his creation. We lose sight of who we're talking to.

And our relationship with him suffers as a result.

3 :: "KEEP HIS COMMANDMENTS, FOR THIS IS THE WHOLE DUTY OF MAN. FOR GOD WILL BRING EVERY DEED INTO JUDGMENT, INCLUDING EVERY HIDDEN THING, WHETHER GOOD OR EVIL" (ECCLESIASTES 12:13-14).

The secret to finding meaning in this life lies with God. Therefore, the only logical thing to do is to obey and follow him. After all he designed the world we're living in. No one knows it as well as he does. So why would we listen to anyone else—including ourselves—in deciding how to live in this world?

Do you have a nice computer? If so how do you treat it? Do you try to take care of it according to the manufacturer's suggestions in the user manual? Or did you say to yourself, "This is my computer, and nobody can tell me what to do with it! Why shouldn't I be able to submerge it in water? It's mine, right? Why shouldn't I write with a permanent marker on the monitor? Why shouldn't I stick lunch meat in the DVD slot? It's mine! It's all mine!"

If you did those things, you would be both right and stupid, wouldn't you? Sure, the computer is yours. And you can do what you want with it. The computer's designers aren't going to come after you to try to stop you. You can ruin the thing if you like.

But if you want to get the best use out of your computer, you'll follow the design instructions.

The same principle applies to you. Your life is yours...in a sense. You can do what you want with it. But if you do the opposite of what the Designer of life tells you to do, you're asking for trouble. For one thing you'll suffer the consequences for mistreating your life. Your life will stop working as it was meant to work. What's more, you'll have to answer to the Designer after your life on earth is all used up.

It's your life—don't be foolish with it.

WHAT SOLOMON DIDN'T KNOW

Solomon was a wise man. The wisest who ever lived. Ecclesiastes 12:9-12 tells us he was a great teacher and a legendary searcher. His knowledge was breathtaking. His calculations were awesome. Everything he wrote was true. And in the book of Ecclesiastes, he's led us on a remarkable journey.

But now we've reached the limit of Solomon's knowledge. You see, we have access to knowledge and truth that Solomon never could have imagined. We have access to the rest of the story.

The apostle Paul has already weighed in several times throughout this book. Now we're going to turn to him for the real conclusion to Solomon's quest. In order to make the most of our short, short lives under the sun, we need to understand four basic principles that God revealed to Paul.

I :: WE FEEL EMPTY FOR A REASON.

The groaning...the sense of longing...the feeling that something is missing in life—it all started a long time ago when two very lonely people walked out of paradise.

Before they sinned Adam and Eve walked with God in the Garden of Eden. They lived with him—in his physical presence. They were able to do that because they were without sin. Remember, God cannot be where sin is, and sin cannot be where God is. So when Adam and Eve sinned, they had to leave God's presence.

That created a tremendous problem for them. You see, human beings are designed by God to be with him. That's what we were built for. We're not meant to be apart from our Creator. That emptiness that Adam and Eve felt...that Solomon felt...that I feel...that you feel...is the human heart longing to be with God.

No wonder everything Solomon tried failed. Sex is no replacement for being with God. All the money and power in the world can't fill a person's longing to be hand-in-hand with the Creator. Even the good gifts God gives us can't take the place of being with him in person—as we are meant to be. Family, friends, wisdom, and enjoying the moment are all good things that can never take away our groaning for God.

2 :: JESUS IS THE ONLY WAY FOR US TO BE WITH GOD.

Jesus left little room for doubt on that point. Look at his words in John 14:6: "I am the way and the truth and the life. No one comes to the Father except through me." You will never be reunited with God—and the emptiness in your soul will never be filled—until you trust Jesus to bridge the gap for you.

His death on the cross paid for your sin. His resurrection destroyed death's power over you. If you believe in him—if you trust him as your Savior and Lord—you will find the intimacy with God that your heart aches for. Not just during your time on earth but for eternity in heaven. Jesus offers the only path that will ultimately give our lives meaning and take away our groaning.

3 :: CHRISTIANS STILL GROAN, AND PART OF US STILL FEELS EMPTY, BECAUSE WE'RE NOT WITH GOD YET.

Imagine those words in giant neon letters. Let them leap off the page and burrow to the center of your brain. They're *that* important.

You see, too many believers have fallen for a terrible, terrible lie. We convince ourselves—or allow ourselves to be convinced—that becoming a Christian will automatically take away all of our emptiness. Some of us actually believe that Christians should never feel the groaning or emptiness Solomon was trying to escape.

But that's not the way it works. Perhaps the most famous Christian of all time wrote these words in Romans 8:22-24:

> We know that the whole creation has been groaning as in the pains of childbirth right up to the present time. Not only so, but we ourselves, who have the firstfruits of the Spirit, groan inwardly as we wait eagerly for our adoption as sons, the redemption of our bodies. For in this hope we were saved.

The apostle Paul felt the painful groaning to be with God in person—after he became a Christian. After the Holy Spirit came into his life. In fact here's a little secret: The emptiness and longing we feel for God might actually get worse for believers the longer we follow Jesus.

That news may be unsettling for some Christians. The emptiness they feel may cause them to believe they're doing something wrong. They may tell themselves if they read their Bible more often...or pray more intently...or develop a purer thought life, their emptiness will disappear. But it won't happen. Those occasional pangs of emptiness and longing won't disappear until we reach our eternal home.

4 :: OUR HOPE IS IN HEAVEN.

If you've ever seen the movie *Field of Dreams,* you'll remember there's a running joke, in which the not-dead-anymore baseball players keep mistaking an Iowa cornfield for heaven. If that seems like a strange way to imagine heaven, check out Paul's words in 2 Corinthians 5:2-6:

> Meanwhile we groan, longing to be clothed with our heavenly dwelling, because when we are clothed, we will not be found naked. For while we are in this tent, we groan and are burdened, because we do not wish to be unclothed but to be clothed with our heavenly dwelling, so that what is mortal may be swallowed up by life.

According to Paul, life on this side of heaven is nothing more than a flimsy tent. A tent so flimsy, that it makes us feel naked and exposed. That's why we long for heaven. We want that safe, secure, and comfortable feeling that comes from being clothed.

What's more, Paul continues ...

> Now it is God who has made us for this very purpose and has given us the Spirit as a deposit, guaranteeing what is to come. Therefore we are always confident and know that as long as we are at home in the body we are away from the Lord.

God made you for one ultimate purpose: to be with him in heaven. As long as you're still here on earth, your groaning will continue. But God has done something to ease that groaning. He's given you his Holy Spirit as a promise that you'll be home soon.

That's a gift Solomon never got to experience or enjoy. God's Spirit works in us to give us love, joy, peace, patience, kindness, goodness, faithfulness, gentleness, and self-control that we wouldn't experience otherwise (see Galatians 5:22-23). He counsels us when we face tough decisions. He assists us in understanding God's Word. He helps us pray. He gives us comfort and power. But he doesn't quench our longing for heaven.

According to Paul the only way to deal with our longing is to look beyond this world. Here's how he explains it in Colossians 3:1-4:

> Since, then, you have been raised with Christ, set your hearts on things above, where Christ is seated at the right hand of God. Set your minds on things above, not on earthly things. For you died, and your life is now hidden with Christ in God. When Christ, who is your life, appears, then you also will appear with him in glory.

The only thing worthy of our mental and emotional hope is life in heaven. Paul encourages us to indulge our longing for our eternal home and the God who will share it with us. Your life now is hidden in heaven with Jesus. Your life starts for real when you get there. It's what you were made for.

Here's what believers who want to experience lasting meaning in life do: They hope in heaven. They don't expect to find any satisfaction in this life—not even by being the best Christians ever. And certainly not in partying, money, or power. Heaven is our only hope of being completely satisfied.

THE REAL PLACE

In order to keep your focus where it needs to be as a believer, you need to live as though heaven is a real place—and not just an abstract theological concept. You also need to live in a way that prepares you for the judgment that awaits you in heaven.

Paul gives us a heads-up in 2 Corinthians 5:9-10:

> So we make it our goal to please him, whether we are at home in the body or away from it. For we must all appear before the judgment seat of Christ, that each one may receive what is due him for the things done while in the body, whether good or bad.

The "judgment seat of Christ" Paul describes in this passage is not the same as the "great white throne judgment" we read about in the book of Revelation. The only people gathered at this judgment are believers who have their names written in the Book of Life. Everyone at this judgment will spend eternity in heaven. The judgment in this situation has to do with how we, as believers, spent our time on earth.

Every believer has the same foundation for life on earth: Jesus Christ. He's what we build on from the moment we trust in him for salvation. But Paul makes it clear in 1 Corinthians 3:12-15 that we don't all build with the same materials.

> If any man builds on this foundation using gold, silver, costly stones, wood, hay or straw, his work will be shown for what it is, because the Day will bring it to light. It will be revealed with fire, and the fire will test the quality of each man's work. If what he has built survives, he will receive his reward. If it is burned up, he will suffer loss; he himself will be saved, but only as one escaping through the flames.

The building materials represent the reasons behind what we do in this life. If we live for money, pleasure, or popularity, then we're building with wood, hay, and straw. If we're living for God and setting our hopes on heaven, then we're building with gold, silver, and gems—solid materials.

Perhaps this passage is where the story of the three little pigs came from. Remember that one? The three pigs are building houses. Pigs 1 and 2 are most interested in having a good time, so they use cheap building materials they can assemble quickly. Pig 3 decides to upgrade to brick, which requires a great deal of time and hard work. While Pig 3 is mixing mortar and baking bricks, Pigs 1 and 2 are out together having the time of their lives.

Of course when the windy wolf shows up, the fun disappears. A couple of puffs from Mr. Wolf bring down the houses of the first two pigs. But Pig 3 can't be budged from his brick condo.

Think of the Big Bad Wolf as the fire that tests how we lived our lives on earth. The giant bonfire at the judgment seat of Christ will reveal that many believers lived totally for themselves, instead of for God's purposes. Almost every minute of their lives will be pronounced "meaningless." Those people will still get into heaven because Jesus paid for their sin himself. But what a waste of time their lives will have been!

For others the bonfire will show that they spent their hours living for what really matters. That is they worked, loved, studied, and even played in ways to please God. They invested their moments in serving him. And as a result, a good percentage of their works will pass the test of fire. And they'll be given special rewards for serving God. We'll all be in heaven together, but the faithful people will be recognized, because they refused to live entirely for meaningless things.

Will you be rewarded for the way you lived? Or will it be obvious to everyone gathered that you lived only for yourself? What are you doing with your hours under the sun? (And we don't mean the time you spend at the beach.)

THE END OF MEANINGLESSNESS

In chapter 9 we read about John's vision of the great white throne judgment, when God will pronounce sentence on unbelievers. But that's not all John saw on his field trip to heaven. Look at his description in Revelation 21:3-5:

> And I heard a loud voice from the throne saying, "Now the dwelling of God is with men, and he will live with them. They will be his people, and God himself will be with them and be their God. He will wipe every tear from their eyes. There will be no more death or mourning or crying or pain, for the old order of things has passed away." He who was seated on the throne said, "I am making everything new!" Then he said, "Write this down, for these words are trustworthy and true."

That's the moment when all groaning will suddenly go silent. All feelings of emptiness and longing will end forever. We'll all be exactly as we were designed to be—with the Father in heaven forever. That's the moment Solomon was longing for, though he couldn't exactly describe it in his day.

That's the moment I'm living for. The moment that gives meaning and purpose to my life and the right choices I make. I hope it's the moment you're living for too.

If not...let me know if you ever catch the wind.

HOW TO TALK TO UNBELIEVING FRIENDS ABOUT FINDING ULTIMATE MEANING

This chapter is aimed specifically at believers in Jesus Christ. He's the key to living with purpose on earth and finding meaning in heaven. Still you can use these issues to start conversations with unbelievers about living a life that really matters.

1 :: ASK YOUR FRIENDS ABOUT YOUTH AND OLD AGE.

What do they believe is the best age in life? Seventeen? Thirty? Fifty-two? Eighty? What do they believe is the best way for a person to spend his or her teens and young adult years? Why? Be ready to explain why you think living for God is an important thing to do when you're young. Ask your friends if they ever picture themselves getting really old. If so does that excite or depress them? Why? Where do they hope they'll be by the time they're in their seventies? What do you hope your life will be like at that time?

2 :: ASK YOUR FRIENDS ABOUT THE COMPUTER ANALOGY.

Do your friends agree that people have the right to treat their computers any way they wish? Do they agree that destroying a computer by purposefully "disobeying" the user manual is a stupid thing to do? Ask them how that's different from violating the instructions of life's Designer by doing whatever we want to do.

3 :: ASK YOUR FRIENDS ABOUT THE NAGGING SENSE THAT THERE MUST BE MORE TO LIFE THAN THIS.

Do they feel that way very often? How would they describe that sense of groaning or longing or the feeling that everything is meaningless because something is missing? How would you describe it? Be prepared to explain your belief that the longing won't be completely met until we get to heaven—because we're meant to be with God. Also be prepared to explain that the only way to get to heaven is through Jesus. Ask your friends what they think about the possibility of heaven's existence—and about how someone can get there.

OBSERVATION EXERCISES

1. Don't just take Solomon's word for it. Gather some data for yourself by conducting a few interviews with people in their seventies or eighties. How do they describe the process of aging? How is it different from being young? If it's not too personal, ask them if they have any regrets about how they spent their youth. What are the best things they did when they were young? When did they seriously start remembering God in their lives? Do they wish it had been sooner or later?

2. How do TV shows and movies usually portray heaven? According to those shows and movies, how do people get into heaven? Is Jesus ever mentioned as the only way to get to heaven?

3. Observe your own heart. Have you ever felt that being a Christian should take away the emptiness in your life? What do you think now, after reading this chapter? How does it make you feel to know that we won't be free of longing until we get what we long for—being with God in person in heaven?

4. Bonus: Write down two or three things that have changed in your understanding of life as a result of reading this book. Have you learned anything new about what's worth chasing and what isn't? Have you changed your opinion of work and enjoyment? Have you grown at all in your understanding of what really matters in life? Taking an honest look at your lifestyle, what are you really hoping in—*right this minute*—to bring meaning and satisfaction to your life?

WHAT ABOUT
WHAT ABOUT TODAY?
TODAY?

Chapter 10 seemed like a logical place to stop this book, didn't it? We covered everything we need to know about Solomon's experiment. We learned that those of us who trust in Christ won't stop feeling homesick until we get to heaven. And we discovered that the choices we make in this world are important because they will be judged in the next one.

So why is there a chapter 11?

Because I need more—and I'm guessing you do too.

Don't get me wrong: Everything Solomon had to say about the things of this world is true. Nothing on this side of heaven can satisfy our deepest longing to be with God. Eternity is our only hope for finding that kind of meaning. Therefore, living a life of obedience to our Maker is the only thing that makes sense in this world.

But where does that leave us?

Should we just plan on a life of silent sadness, future hope, and cold obedience? Should we sit around, waiting to die, so we can finally find meaning in heaven? Should we give up any hope for having fun in this world?

No, no, and no.

You see, the reality of Jesus and the hope of heaven can—and should—change the way we live today. As believers we have the opportunity to do more than live a life that matters for eternity. We can also live a life today that's hopeful, wild, full—and fun.

TODAY'S THE DAY

Here are six ways in which the hope of heaven can make a difference in your life right now.

1 :: YOU CAN PHONE HOME.

Or e-mail. Or send smoke signals. Whatever analogy works best for you. The point is even though we may not find ultimate satisfaction until we're with God in heaven, our relationship with him has already begun through our faith in Jesus. And with that relationship comes the privilege of communicating with him. If you'll take advantage of that opportunity, you'll find that God will fill your life with energy, growth, passion, and wonder.

Talking to God in prayer involves more than just filling out a form and dropping it in his inbox. Think of it in terms of opening a live channel to the Creator of the universe. The Father who's adopted us into his family. The connection crackles with supernatural power as his Holy Spirit tells him directly what we *want* to communicate but often don't know how to say (see Romans 8:26-27).

Even more exciting is the fact that prayer is a two-way conversation. God talks to us as well. When we open his Word, the Holy Spirit supernaturally ignites its meaning in our hearts and minds. The words of Scripture work together with the Word (Jesus) to transform us from the inside out. And to make us more and more like him.

2 :: YOU CAN RELAX.

Your friends and neighbors who don't believe in Christ can't stop searching. They're driven to find the one thing that will finally quiet their groaning. Unless they've given up hope completely, they must keep striving to find the answer.

But you can relax. If you can accept the fact that your only hope for true meaning is in heaven, you can call off the search. Bring in the dogs. Stop your constant searching. You can rest. While everyone else runs around, frantically tasting everything life has to offer, you can have some tea.

Part of the peace we find in Jesus is the ability to stop our endless and pointless search for meaning in other things.

Do you have trouble relaxing? Maybe you're holding on to some false hopes that you can find meaning in something in this meaningless life. If so try this: Pick a Scripture passage that will remind you that you've officially given up the search, write it down, memorize it, and spend a little time each day rolling it around between your ears. If you're not sure where to look, start with Proverbs 3:5-6 or Matthew 11:28-30 or 1 Timothy 6:7-8.

3 :: YOU CAN TAKE COMFORT IN THE FACT THAT YOU DON'T HAVE TO BE PERFECT.

The hope of perfect meaning and satisfaction in heaven means you can let go of your quest to be perfect on earth. This is a huge point for some of you. I know who you are—I've seen your eyes in my mirror. You have no problem agreeing that it's a waste of time to look for meaning in partying and sex and getting rich. You nod your head in agreement when we talk about the ultimate pointlessness of laughter and entertainment and building empires.

But you're stuck on something. You still have the idea in the back of your head that if you could just be perfect—or close to it—you could reach some level of satisfaction here on earth. So you drive yourself toward that perfect SAT or GPA. Or you punish your body in search of physical perfection. Or worse, you've turned following Jesus into a chase for spiritual perfection—using prayer, Bible study, and obedience as a system of self-improvement instead of opportunities to walk with God.

The hard truth is you'll never find perfection on this side of heaven. In fact you'll never come close. And thanks to Jesus, you don't have to. In heaven you'll be as perfect as God created you to be. Today you can be satisfied with the fact that God is in the middle of transforming you. And no amount of effort on your part is going to complete the process in the next hour or so.

As for the rest of you...I know you too. You've decided that because you've already blown it so badly—because you've already sinned in some really gross ways or made some really lousy decisions—you might as well not even try to follow Jesus. You figure, *What's the point in trying? I've already failed.*

But here's what you need to understand. No matter what you've done—or haven't done—in the past, you can start walking with Jesus again. Right now. You can make choices today that will matter forever. Don't walk away from the best thing in your life just because you don't feel like the poster child for the American Christian Teenager.

4 :: YOU CAN BE FEARLESS AND CONFIDENT.

Sports commentators always say the hardest teams to beat are the ones with nothing to lose. The team that has no shot at the playoffs—and nothing to play for—isn't restricted by pressure or fear of failure. Its players have the luxury of going all out on every play. They can run, jump, hit, and throw with wild abandon. They have no reason to hold back. They know perfection (or even the next level of success) is beyond their reach—so they can relax and focus on what's in front of them.

For Christians who have put all their hope for ultimate meaning in heaven, life can be like that all the time. Fearless. Confident. Bold.

Think about the things that usually scare us or steal our confidence. The prospect of looking like a fool. Or being rejected. Or not getting accepted by the right college. Or not finding true love.

Then ask yourself...*So what?*

Every worst-case scenario is temporary. As a follower of Christ, you have things no one can take away. The Creator of all is your Father. You will be with him forever. Your groaning and emptiness will be silenced in heaven.

As the apostle Paul explains in 2 Corinthians 5:6, those facts mean you can be "always confident" about your future. The apostle Peter points out you don't have to be afraid of what most people worry about (1 Peter 3:14). You have nothing to lose. So why should you be afraid of making a wrong decision or being rejected by people or looking stupid? Nothing can touch your ultimate future. You can follow God with wild abandon, trying things for him you never thought possible—and sometimes even succeeding.

That's the abundant life Jesus promised to everyone who's willing to let go of the false hopes of this world and live for the real hope of the next world. If you're not fearless—or even confident—right now, that's okay. You're not perfect yet. But you might ask yourself what you're really hoping in. What are you afraid of losing—and why?

"For God did not give us a spirit of timidity, but a spirit of power, of love and of self-discipline" (2 Timothy 1:7).

5 :: YOU CAN LIVE WITH JOY.

Joy is not the same thing as happiness. Happy feelings come and go, often depending on the circumstances of the day. If the sun comes out or my team wins the big game, I'm happy. If I fail the test or get dumped, I'm sad. Standard human emotions.

Joy is an entirely different thing—at least in the way the Bible uses the word. Joy is a powerful confidence inside you that what you're experiencing is right and good. Most people experience joy at certain times in their lives. Perhaps after a hard-fought or unexpected victory. Or at a wedding. Or at the birth of a baby. Or when they're reunited with someone they love very much. Or when something lost is finally found.

That's why joy is such a huge part of the Christian life. In Christ we're promised a great victory over the enemy...a reunion with God and other believers in heaven...a new birth...and the path to ultimate meaning. And it's all going to last forever.

That's a joy Solomon couldn't imagine. He talked about finding joy in the everyday gifts of God—and we do. But those good gifts are just little tastes of the avalanche of goodness that will swallow us up in the forever life of heaven. That's why I can choose to live with joy. Even if things in this world look very dark, heaven is just around the corner.

The women who went to take care of Jesus' body on the first Easter morning and found it missing were said to be afraid—but filled with joy! (Matthew 28:8) So as unlikely as it seems, fear and joy can exist together.

Likewise, Jesus describes how even in the pain of childbirth, joy can come out on top because of new life (John 16:21). In the next verse, he makes it clear his followers will be given great joy that no one can take away.

Paul says even in his worst troubles, his joy couldn't be boxed up (2 Corinthians 7:4). And he expresses over and over the joy he felt when he hung out with other believers who were hoping in heaven for their ultimate meaning. As believers we have that joy built into us, thanks to God's Holy Spirit.

That doesn't mean we'll always act joyful—or even feel joyful, for that matter. However, we can always choose to *be* joyful—even when we don't feel it—because of Jesus and the hope of heaven. In fact we're commanded to "be joyful in hope" (Romans 12:12).

James says being joyful is a choice you make concerning where you put your hope. If you choose to hope that heaven is your home—and give up your hope in the dead ends of this life—then you can call even the worst days joyful because they bring you a step closer to your ultimate destination (James 1:2).

If you know you'll find everything you're looking for on the streets of heaven, you don't have to give up joy—even when you experience sorrow in the back alleys of earth. The Holy Spirit's joy is always with you.

6 :: YOU CAN SHARE THE SECRET.

Peter lived in a hard time for Christians. First-century believers were regularly persecuted and killed for what they believed. From the outside looking in, things often looked hopeless for the early church. But not to Peter. Look at his bold words in 1 Peter 3:14-15:

> "Do not fear what they fear; do not be frightened." But in your hearts set apart Christ as Lord. Always be prepared to give an answer to everyone who asks you to give the reason for the hope that you have. But do this with gentleness and respect.

Peter expected people to notice something different about believers. He expected them to ask Christ's followers how they could be so hopeful, given their terrible circumstances. They were being tortured and killed, after all. Families were being torn apart. Awful things were happening.

But Peter knew the hope of heaven changes people in dramatic ways. It makes them able to reject fear—even when it makes perfect sense to be afraid. It allows them to respond to dire circumstances in a relaxed, confident, and joyful way.

Peter wanted his readers to be ready when the questions came. He wanted God's people to be prepared to share the secret to living with hope. It's a secret Solomon never knew. But if you're a Christian, you know it.

The question is: Are you ready to share it? What will you say if someone asks, "How can you be so hopeful after everything you've been through?" or "Why are you so positive all the time?" or "How can you be so confident?"

Will you be ready to talk about the reason for your hope? About Jesus? About the end of meaninglessness on that day in heaven when all who trust in Christ will find themselves home?

THE REAL, ACTUAL, FINAL CONCLUSION

Where are you hoping to find meaning, purpose, and joy today? What do you expect to fill the longing in your heart? What are you willing to sacrifice in order to get that thing? Do you believe it will pay off in the long run?

My prayer for you as you close this book is that you'll be courageous enough to ask yourself those hard questions today, tomorrow, next week, and throughout your life. And that you'll have the double courage to trust God enough to come up with honest answers. Please don't waste your life re-running Solomon's great experiment. You know the results. Live for what matters.

HOW TO TALK TO UNBELIEVING FRIENDS ABOUT THE HOPE OF HEAVEN

For unbelieving friends and family members, this chapter is where the rubber of your stated beliefs meets the road of what they see in your day-to-day life. And believe me, they're paying attention.

1 :: ASK YOUR FRIENDS ABOUT CHRISTIANS THEY'VE OBSERVED UP CLOSE AND PERSONAL.

Do they notice any real difference between people who do or don't claim to have hope in heaven through faith in Jesus? Do the Christians they know personally seem to have more peace, joy, confidence, fearlessness, or any of the other qualities the Bible attaches to walking with Jesus? If your friends have noticed differences, how do they explain them? Do they see them as evidence of the reality of faith in God? As evidence of the power of God himself? Why or why not?

2 :: ASK YOUR FRIENDS ABOUT THEIR LIVES.

Do they feel relaxed, confident, hopeful, fearless, joyful, and at peace? If so to what do they attribute those qualities? If not do they want to experience those things? What would they be willing to do in order to attain those qualities?

3 :: GET SPECIFIC ABOUT JESUS.

Ask your friends what they think about Christianity—in general and for them specifically. Would they ever consider trusting in Jesus alone for salvation from sin and the hope of finding ultimate meaning in heaven? What would keep them from making such a commitment? What else in life do they hope will bring them peace, contentment, joy, confidence, fearlessness, and meaning?

What could you do to help them move closer to making a commitment to Christ?

OBSERVATION EXERCISES

1. Write down the names of three or four Christians in your life who seem to live in close relationship with God...who seem to have stopped searching for meaning in this life...who don't seem desperate to be perfect on their own...who project confidence instead of fear...and who seem to live in joy. Is it hard to name Christians like that in your world? If so why do you think that is? Talk to one of the people on your list about your perceptions. Ask him or her where those qualities come from.

2. Think of the people in your life whose spiritual beliefs are a mystery to you. Do you notice in any of them a sense of peace, joy, or hopefulness that makes you believe they're putting their hope in heaven? Are there others you'd draw the opposite conclusion about? Consider asking one or two of them about the reason for their hopefulness.

3. Observe your own heart. It's one thing to read a book like this and agree with the ideas about placing your hope in heaven and not in all of the other things people chase in their search for meaning. It's another thing to actually give up the search and settle your "hope fully on the grace to be given" in heaven (1 Peter 1:13). How many of these qualities do you see in your own life: peace, joyfulness, hopefulness, confidence and fearlessness because of your future with God, love for other believers, a freedom from endless searching for meaning in this life? If some of those qualities seem to be missing in your life, why do you think that is? Have you not yet committed fully to resting in Christ alone to as the source of all meaning? If not what would it take for you to do so?